Spiritually Single

Living with an Unbelieving Husband

Jeri Odell

Beacon Hill Press of Kansas City
Kansas City, Missouri

Copyright 2002
by Jeri Odell

ISBN 083-411-9730

Printed in the
United States of America

Cover Design: Michael Walsh

Library of Congress Cataloging-in-Publication Data

Odell, Jeri, 1956-
    Spiritually single : living with an unbelieving husband / Jeri Odell.
      p. cm.
    ISBN 0-8341-1973-0 (pbk.)
    1. Wives—Religious life. 2. Christian women—Religious life. 3. Husbands—Religious
life. 4. Non church-affiliated people—Family relationships. I. Title.
    BV4528.15 .O34 2002
    248.8'435—dc21

                                                          2002004417

10   9   8   7   6   5   4   3   2   1

This book is written for you, my sisters in Christ. My 20-year journey as an unequally yoked Christian woman has left me with many memories to share. Some of those are sad, some happy; all carry the fingerprints of Christ. I pray that you'll see Him in each life lesson, for without Jesus I would have no story to tell, no victory to claim.

My hope is that you'll avoid the mistakes I've made. I recently read this quote: "If you can't be a good example, then you'll just have to be a horrible warning." Please heed my warning, learn from my failures, and do it right the first time.

In His amazing, healing, life-changing love,
Jeri

Dean,

I love you. Thanks for staying when leaving would have been easier. As I write this book, I feel amazed and humbled that you put up with me for all these years.

Forever and a day,
Me

Contents

Wives, in the same way be submissive to your husbands so that, if any of them do not believe the word, they may be won over without words by the behavior of their wives, when they see the purity and reverence of your lives (1 Pet. 3:1-2).

1

You Grow, Girl!
Don't Wait—for Tomorrow May Never Come

I headed for my favorite pew—third from the front on the left side of the sanctuary. As I waited for the service to begin, I flipped through the bulletin. Church training classes for the fall semester were scheduled to start next week. I read over the synopsis of each class, not intending to participate because I was waiting for my husband, Dean. Once he made a commitment to Christ, we would grow together.

You could wait forever, my conscience nagged. After all, I had already delayed the process three years. *I'm terrified to go on without him. If I mature in the Lord, the chasm between us will only expand.* Going forward with God would only make the "great divide" greater.

It's time, a still, small voice whispered. I pushed the thought out of my mind and stood for the opening song. A lump lodged in my throat. *Do I have the strength to do this alone?* I glanced at my eight-year-old son, Matt, and five-year-old daughter, Kelsy, and thought of three-year-old Adam playing in the nursery. *For their sakes I have to make spiritual growth a priority.*

Sounds so easy now, but it was truly one of the toughest life decisions I had made up to that point. For the previous three years I had faithfully attended church but sensed God wanted more, so I jumped into this faith walk with both feet. No more waiting. Just God and I would embark on this journey. "I Have Decided to Follow Jesus" became my theme song, and to this day I can't get through the third verse without tears: "Tho' none go with me, still I will follow; / No turning back, no turning back."

GROWING WITH GOD

The following Sunday evening I showed up for my pastor's class titled "The Principles of Spiritual Growth." I made a commitment to God and myself—this girl would grow. I traded in my five-minute morning devotions for a deeper Bible study that had me digging into the Word for answers and life application. I asked God to teach me to pray—really pray—and I increased my church involvement by not only taking a Sunday evening class but also signing on for a ladies' midweek Bible study.

Dean is my priority above church and second only to God. When I honor my husband, I honor God.

I'm not implying that increased involvement in church activity alone induces growth. I'm not advocating for the church to dominate your life. I carefully added a couple of endeavors to my schedule that would draw me closer to Christ through the study of His Word. I constantly pray for wisdom and sensitivity on how involved I should be, since my husband isn't. Dean is my priority above church and second only to God. When I honor my husband, I honor God. If he ends up resenting either God or church, nobody benefits.

My friend Ellen* had to choose less involvement to keep her homelife peaceful. Having made a childhood

---

*Some names in this book have been changed.

commitment to Christ, Ellen married during a period in her life when Jesus seemed unimportant. Later, she returned to the Lord. Problem is, her husband, David, resents her Christianity and sometimes even mocks her faith. She strives to maintain harmony in their home by attending church only on Sunday mornings and staying home with him in the evenings. She reads her Bible while he's at work to avoid confrontation.

"We're called to live at peace with everyone, including our unbelieving spouses, which can require extra effort on our part," Ellen says. "We all have to find what works best in our individual situation. There's no magic formula, but God will help supply the right answers if we ask."

That said, don't be afraid to grow. Looking back, I realize my growth has enhanced our marriage and didn't hinder our relationship, as I originally presumed it would. When I put God first, He changed my heart toward Dean. God used Paul's advice to the Colossians to challenge me: "Whatever you do, work at it with all your heart, as working for the Lord, not for men" (3:23). God was asking me to put my whole heart into my marriage—for Him.

Lori, a friend at church, shared with me what God taught her during a difficult period in her marriage. "Regardless of what Steve did or didn't do, regardless of his salvation status, and regardless of his contribution to the relationship, God expected my best. Marriage isn't a 50/50 proposition, but rather my giving my 100 percent."

Those words have haunted, rebuked, and blessed me many times over the years. She's right. When I stand before God, I long to hear Him say, "Well done, thou good and faithful wife." I don't desire to stand before Him blaming Dean for my shortcomings. "But, God, I didn't because he didn't . . ." Those words won't carry much weight with the Almighty.

The spiritual condition of my spouse doesn't change my role except to create a more vital need for obedience to Scripture. As Peter reminds me, the unbeliever will be won over by the behavior—not the words—of his believing mate. Even more reason to grow. How can I practice what I do not know? And how can I know unless I grow in my knowledge of God?

Prov. 31 paints the epitome of a godly woman, yet never states whether her husband practiced faith. With so little revealed about him, I must surmise his spiritual condition held no relevance to her role as a godly wife, nor does my husband's for me.

So I pass the gauntlet on to you. It's with love, hope, and prayers I say, "You grow, girl!" Move toward God with passionate fervor. Don't wait for anyone or anything. May God bless you as you grow in Him!

MY STORY

As a little girl, I grew up attending Sunday School and church. I invited Jesus into my heart at a fairly young age, but when I was about 10 years old, my family traded our Sundays at church for weekends following the junior rodeo circuit around the state of Arizona.

I left God in my past with pigtails, skinned knees, and Barbies while I moved forward into a new life with new friends and new ideas.

I left God in my past with pigtails, skinned knees, and Barbies while I moved forward into a new life with new friends and new ideas. At the ripe old age of 15, I met my future husband, Dean. He sure looked good in his Wranglers, Tony Lama Ropers, and a Stetson perched on his head. His blue eyes drew my interest, and his smile sent my heart into overdrive. The fact he had no relationship with Jesus Christ mattered little.

Not too many years later, we said, "I do." Life was good. We started having kids, and we owned a house and a new car. What more could a girl want?

Then on a Friday morning in February, I got a call that caused me to reevaluate my entire life and the direction I was headed.

"Dad's dead." My younger brother's voice carried a couple of thousand miles over the phone line.

"He's gone," Kenny continued softly. "He went out to feed the horses and never came back. He had a massive heart attack and died right there in the corral."

During the following days, I knew beyond a doubt that God wanted my attention, and for the first time in years, He had it. As I held each of my three preschoolers, I realized I desired for them to grow up knowing God, learning the same Bible stories I had learned as a child, and I wanted the assurance that when they died, heaven would be their eternal home. As James Dobson asks, "Will you be there?" How *could* they be if they never heard?

My dad's death was both the worst and best event that had occurred in my 20-something years on earth. I would miss him terribly, but I sensed a great turning point in my life and my kids' lives.

The Sunday after his funeral and most Sundays since, I've been in church. My kids grew up in a church family, with a church home, and each one of them has made a profession of faith in Jesus. I'm so thankful to God for intervening in my life while my children were still young and pliable. There are worse things in life than growing up without a grandpa—they could have grown up without a Savior.

In Summary

Growth isn't easy; God's pruning is sometimes painful. But since I'm His, He'll continue bringing circumstances into my life to conform me to the image of His precious Son, just as He promised in Phil. 1:6—"Being confident of this, that he who began a good work in you will carry it on to completion until the day of Christ Jesus." His goal is for me to become more and more like His Son, but the choice is ultimately mine as to whether I allow situations in my life to push me toward God or away from Him. Making the right choice is a matter of prayer.

God's pruning is sometimes painful. But since I'm His, He'll continue bringing circumstances into my life to conform me to the image of His precious Son.

Let's look at examples from Scripture: one man embraced growth and hardship; the others cared only about outward appearances. First consider Paul, originally known as Saul, who persecuted Christians with fervor. Traveling to Damascus to take more Christian prisoners back to Jerusalem, he came face-to-face with the living, loving Lord Jesus Christ:

Suddenly a light from heaven flashed around him. He fell to the ground and heard a voice say to him, "Saul, Saul, why do you persecute me?"

"Who are you, Lord?" Saul asked.

"I am Jesus, whom you are persecuting," he replied. "Now get up and go into the city, and you will be told what you must do" *(Acts 9:3-6).*

From then on, Paul served Jesus with the same fervor he had previously used to oppose Him. Paul faced more hardships throughout his life than most of us will ever come close to enduring, and yet His love for Christ only grew stronger. He gave up his prestigious position as a Jewish Pharisee to grow in the grace and the knowledge of our Lord and Savior.

Paul is a man who considered spiritual growth not just imperative, but a privilege. In his letter to the Philippians he wrote, "Whatever was to my profit I now consider loss for the sake of Christ. What is more, I consider everything a loss compared to the surpassing greatness of knowing Christ Jesus my Lord, for whose sake I have lost all things. I consider them rubbish, that I may gain Christ and be found in him" (3:7-9). Oh, to be found in Him—the very cry of my heart!

Paul goes on to write in verse 10, "I want to know Christ and the power of his resurrection and the fellowship of sharing in his sufferings, becoming like him in his death." Whatever the cost would be, Paul deemed knowing Christ worth it.

Now let's contrast the life of Paul with the lives of the Pharisees. They were a group of Jewish men who placed great importance on rites and tradition rather than in a personal, growing relationship with God. Always much more concerned with appearances than with the true condition of their hearts, these men made a point of praying more loudly, making the tassels on their prayer shawls longer, and wearing the widest phylacteries. But Christ exposed them for what they really were.

The dissimilarity is amazing. Paul started the same way they started, a Pharisee in his own right. But his life took a much different turn when he chose to make Jesus his Lord. Relationships don't just sit still—they're either growing and moving forward or dying and stagnating. I yearn to be like Paul, living a thriving, exciting, Christ-filled life. How about you?

PONDERING GOD'S WORD

Do more than read the following scriptures—pray them, think about them, and hide them in your heart.

- "We will in all things grow up into him who is the Head, that is, Christ" (Eph. 4:15).
- "Your faith is growing more and more, and the love every one of you has for each other is increasing" (2 Thess. 1:3).
- "Let us leave the elementary teachings about Christ and go on to maturity" (Heb. 6:1).
- "Like newborn babies, crave pure spiritual milk, so that by it you may grow up in your salvation" (1 Pet. 2:2).
- "Grow in the grace and knowledge of our Lord and Savior Jesus Christ" (2 Pet. 3:18).

Father God,

Give me the desire to know You, to seek first Your kingdom and Your righteousness and to hunger and thirst for You alone. I pray spiritual growth will always be a priority in my life and that I'll take every opportunity to know You better. Give me a deep love for Your Word and a passion for prayer.

May I never confuse church activity with growth, and may I never make church attendance more important than my husband. Enable me to put my whole heart into being a wife so that You might receive glory. Though none go with me, give me the strength, courage, and tenacity never to turn back, to keep moving forward with You by my side.

I thank You for the privilege of knowing You and being Your child. I'm always in awe that You—God most holy, God most high—allow me to enter into Your presence and sit at Your feet. May I never take for granted Your open invitation to meet You in the holy of holies. I love You and am so grateful You love me back. Thank You. I pray in the awesome name of Jesus Christ. Amen.

Listening to God's Voice

List some areas in which God is asking you to grow.

_____

_____

_____

_____

_____

_____

_____

_____

_____

_____

_____

_____

_____

_____

_____

_____

2

He Jumped Ship
Hanging On to Faith
When He Doesn't

"Bill's getting worse and worse," Sarah confessed to me several years ago at lunch. "He actually denied the existence of God the other night at dinner." The sadness of Sarah's countenance reflected the grief in her voice.

I had no words, but my heart ached for her. I assumed it would be even more difficult to have a Christian husband and see him jump ship than never to have had a believing husband at all. After all, Sarah had a taste of sharing her faith walk with her spouse but now had to give it up.

Sighing, she continued. "He's reduced God to a mere myth—a crutch for the weak. What happened to my Christian husband? Where did he go?" Pain reverberated through her questions.

I shook my head, having no idea. Spiritual singleness is a difficult role, and unfortunately, churches everywhere include married people who walk alone in their commitment to Christ. Their spouses either lack devotion or don't believe. Worse yet, some face mocking in their own home by the very person who vowed to love them for better or worse. No matter how any of us got into these unequally yoked relationships, the pain is similar.

After placing our orders with the waitress, Sarah continued: "I've wondered so many times what happened.

Even as a child I was determined to marry a Christian. I honestly thought I had. He told me he had accepted Christ as his Savior as a child at Vacation Bible School. Did I miss something?"

She felt cheated, having married one guy and ending up with quite another. Somewhere along the way, Bill's faith sprouted wings and took flight.

"While we were dating, we prayed together, seeking God's will and blessing. After we got married and moved to Phoenix, the first thing we did was get involved at a Bible-believing church. We were baptized together and attended Sunday School regularly." Tears filled her eyes as she remembered.

Our iced teas arrived, giving Sarah a moment to compose herself.

"Doesn't he still attend church with you?"

"Yes, but sometimes I wish he didn't. His critical comments and negative attitudes affect my ability to worship. There are times I just want to crawl under the pew and hide because of some cynical statement he said loud enough to be heard in six counties."

"I'm sorry," I responded. "I know it's hard. You don't have a clue what caused his about-face?"

"I could make a guess. I think he assumed that doing the right thing automatically leads to blessing. He seemed to expect life to roll smoothly along and our three boys to make no mistakes. As you can guess, neither happened. Our kids didn't always make the best choices, and I think he may have become disillusioned."

As we ate salad, Sarah continued. "When the boys were in high school, Bill commented that he didn't see any difference between being a Christian and not. He said, 'Everybody has the same problems, no miracles happen for anyone, and Christians aren't given special protection. If there's a God, why do people suffer?' I thought it was a phase, only it hasn't phased out, but instead he's grown more skeptical with time."

Sarah and I parted that day with my wishing I had answers to her tough problem. Sadly, I didn't. But I knew God did!

RENEWED HOPE

Recently when I was in Phoenix for a conference, Sarah and I met again for lunch. I was encouraged by her growth and the truths God had taught Sarah during the years since I'd seen her. We can all learn from what God taught Sarah. I love the old adage "A wise man learns from the mistakes of others, a man learns from his own mistakes, and a fool never learns." My prayer is for each of us to be wise, gleaning from one another.

After a hug, Sarah and I followed the hostess to a corner table. We shared some small talk as we looked at the menu and placed our orders. Then Sarah jumped in, sharing the answers God had provided for her.

"I grappled with how and why life turned out this way and many other hard questions for several years," Sarah said.

"What other questions?"

"Well, I doubted myself. I wondered if I subconsciously knew all along that Bill wasn't a Christian and just desperately wanted him to be. Was this turn of events somehow my fault? Had I been unwilling to wait for God's choice? I was ready for marriage, so did I forge ahead without God's blessing? I pondered tough issues with no concrete or easy answers.

"God finally told me it didn't matter. Bill is my husband, and he is God's will and God's plan for me now. Whether or not I made a huge mistake in marrying Bill is irrelevant. God led me to 1 Cor. 7:17—'Each one should retain the place in life that the Lord assigned to him and to which God has called him.' My place in life is Bill's wife, and God is calling me to be the best Bill's wife I can be.

"God is sovereign, and I believe He promises in Romans 8:28 that this, too, will work for my good. I can already see it has. My relationship with Him has grown, and He's so dear to me now. That didn't happen when Bill was playing Christian. I'm a follower and was content to trail behind Bill along the road of mediocre Christianity, so God has drawn me into a deeper relationship with Him in the midst of my husband's abandoning the faith.

It's not my job to change or convince my husband of his misguided ways. God's Holy Spirit is in charge of conviction, not me.

"In many aspects, I had made Bill an idol in my life. He had my love, my devotion, my trust. As crazy as it sounds, I've even grown closer to Bill because of my thriving, growing love for the Lord. Bill no longer has to meet all my needs and live up to all my expectations. After I worked through all the hurt, anger, and bitterness, I freed Bill to just be my husband. Whether he's a believer or not, I'm to love him. And now I can!"

"Wow—you've come a long way!" I said. I was amazed at the transformation.

"God can work miracles in our hearts if we let Him," Sarah responded. "Another thing He taught me through those dark days was that it's not my job to change or convince my husband of his misguided ways. God's Holy Spirit is in charge of conviction, not me. I'm not responsible for the choices Bill makes; he alone is accountable to God for his choices.

"However, I'm responsible to pray for him, and God is

teaching me to use Scripture as I lift my husband before God's throne of grace. Another responsibility I have is to reveal Christ by allowing Him to fill me, change me, and empower me. God has shown me that Bill is open to seeing what God is teaching me as I share in a noncondemning, nonjudgmental kind of way. He doesn't desire to hear my opinions or my doctrine, but he *is* interested in my personal relationship with Christ and how that plays into my daily choices. I believe these opportunities are gifts from God, and I strive to remember that I'm the aroma of God—so I'm to act like it!"

"Why is it we act the least godly around those we love the most?" I asked. After a few bites in silence, I asked, "Does he still go to church with you?"

"Yes, and you know, that's still the hardest thing. He no longer wants to go to Sunday School or get involved, so I'm not plugged in either. It's a lost, lonely feeling. I attend a women's midweek Bible study, and that helps. I almost envy you getting to go alone and not having the pressure of a negative, critical man with you."

"And I envy *you* because I'd take him any way I could get him if he'd just go to church!"

"The grass always looks greener, doesn't it?" Sarah asked.

It sure does, but it rarely is.

FREEDOM FOUND

I appreciate the truths Sarah shared that day. I value her insights about true freedom being found in letting go of our husbands and placing them in God's trustworthy hands. It took almost 20 years for me to get a clue.

When I finally did learn to trust God with Dean and make the most of our marriage by enjoying it and him, enormous freedom followed. Finally, instead of my faith tripping us up, it now enhances our relationship. Dean carries the title of "friend," which wasn't always true. God is teaching me to love him unconditionally and to accept him just as he is and just where he is. It's God's job to change him.

Liberty comes also in realizing and accepting this marriage as God's good and perfect will for my life. He's not surprised or caught off guard at how my choices played out. I must let go of past mistakes and make the most of today. Regrets serve no purpose other than to weigh me down and keep my faith from soaring. In Him, any hardship can strengthen my faith walk.

The fragrance of Christ should be so evident that the fruit of His presence in me touches my home, family, and husband constantly.

I appreciate Sarah's challenge for each of us to be the aroma of Christ in our husband's life. In all honesty, I'm often not. What a great lesson to learn and put into practice! After I searched God's Word, this is what I discovered about being the sweet fragrance of Jesus: He should be discernible in me to both the saved and unsaved and certainly to my own husband. It should be obvious to anyone who meets me that I belong to God. I wonder if it is. Even more important, is it obvious to Dean?

I thought a lot about an aroma and how it permeates a room and often a whole house. I love candles, and burning just one fills the room with fragrance. The scent often spills over into adjacent rooms of the house. Baking has the same effect. Walk through my front door when I'm baking manicotti, and my entire home is filled with the bouquet of oregano, basil, and garlic.

The same should be true of me. The fragrance of
Christ should be so evident that the fruit of his presence
in me touches my home, family, and husband constantly.
His presence is substantiated by the manifestation of the
Holy Spirit in my life through the fruit spoken of in Gal.
5:22-23: "Love, joy, peace, patience, kindness, goodness,
faithfulness, gentleness and self-control" are confirmation
that my life bears the aroma of Jesus.

SCRIPTURAL EXAMPLES

I prayerfully sought two contrasting examples from
Scripture to illustrate the whole idea of jumping ship. The
first, Jonah, ran from God for a while but then returned
and obeyed. The second, Demas, abandoned the call and
as far as we know never looked back.

Jonah was one of the early prophets and is known as
the reluctant missionary. You probably remember the story
from childhood. God called Jonah to go to Nineveh, the
famed capital of the ancient Assyrian Empire, and announce His judgment against them. Jonah said, "Thanks,
but no thanks," and skipped out on God's assignment. He
literally headed in the opposite direction, bought a ticket,
and caught a ship heading west to escape the Lord.

Now, I don't know about you, but I've tried to escape
the Lord a few times myself, and it never works. It didn't
work for Jonah either. Once they were at sea, the Lord sent
a violent storm that threatened the lives of all aboard. The
crew, in hopes of finding the culprit, cast lots to see who
among them had offended the gods. Jonah lost the toss.
He told them to throw him overboard to calm the wind,
and after every other attempt failed, they did just that.

The Lord sent a great fish to swallow Jonah, and he
resided in the fish's belly three days and three nights.
While there, he cried out to God, promising to fulfill all

his vows. The next time the Lord sent Jonah to Nineveh, after the fish had deposited him on the beach, he obeyed.

Some abandon their faith for a season, as Jonah did, but it seems some never return. Demas, one of Paul's co-laborers, worked beside him on at least one missionary journey. He's mentioned in the Bible only three times, and two of those times he sent greetings and salutations. But the third time Paul penned Demas's name, he wrote, "Do your best to come to me quickly, for Demas, because he loved this world, has deserted me and has gone to Thessalonica" (2 Tim. 4:9-10). His love for the world drew his heart away from serving God, and in the process it sounds as though he left Paul in a bind.

I'm not sure why, but I find those two short verses deeply moving. How many of us have known fellow faith walkers who suddenly veered off the path? My heart aches for them as they fall in love with the things of this world, searching for fulfillment in empty answers when everything they ever needed was theirs in Christ.

Don't be fooled. This world can never offer us true peace, contentment, or the joy that Jesus brings. His joy isn't based on circumstances, but on His presence in our lives. I just walked with a close friend through the death of her 24-year-old son, Brian. Leukemia claimed his body but couldn't touch his soul. Even facing death and saying good-bye to his wife and family couldn't rob Brian of the joy of the Lord. This world had no hold on him, and I realized at his funeral that if God measured our lives by the people we touch with His love rather than by years, Brian died a very old man. May God find me just as faithful.

PONDERING GOD'S WORD

- "Being confident of this, that he who began a good work in you [or your husband] will carry it on to completion until the day of Christ Jesus" (Phil. 1:6).
- "Let us throw off everything that hinders and the sin

that so easily entangles, and let us run with persever-
ance the race marked out for us" (Heb. 12:1).

- "I have fought the good fight, I have finished the
  race, I have kept the faith" (2 Tim. 4:7).
- "I consider my life worth nothing to me, if only I may
  finish the race and complete the task the Lord Jesus
  has given me—the task of testifying to the gospel of
  God's grace" (Acts 20:24).
- "One thing I do: Forgetting what is behind and
  straining toward what is ahead, I press on toward
  the goal" (Phil. 3:13-14).

Father,

*I come to You with a grateful heart, knowing that when things
seem hopeless, as they did for Sarah, You renew my hope and give
me the strength and courage to carry on. Whatever I face, if I give
You permission, You will use it for good in my life. Help me to remember that promise and claim it when I need to.*

*I thank You for the freedom that came when I let go of things I
couldn't control anyway. I don't need to fret over yesterday's mistakes or worry about the crises tomorrow may hold—I just need to
rest in You today. May I press on toward the goal of knowing You
more intimately.*

*Lord, I confess I need work in the area of being permeated with
the sweet fragrance of Jesus. My odor is often the scent of selfish-
ness, nagging, or disappointment. How much I want to be the
sweet fragrance of Jesus instead! How desperately I hope to touch
with You each person I encounter. Change me, Lord, until all Dean
sees when he looks at me is Christ. It's in His precious, worthy
name I pray. Amen.*

Listening to God's Voice

What is God saying to you about your responsibility to
your husband?

_____

_____

_____

_____

_____

_____

_____

_____

_____

_____

_____

_____

_____

_____

_____

3

Surrendered at Last!
When He Doesn't Give All to Jesus

Hurt and betrayed by her first husband, Julie didn't intend to get into another relationship. As a romance novelist, she had told more than one well-meaning friend who tried to fix her up, "I'll keep my men in my books. Then when they misbehave, all I have to do is press 'delete.'" If only life were that simple.

A chance meeting at her apartment's swimming pool weakened her resolve. After a bad day at work, she had planned to swim a few laps, work off some stress—but a mutual acquaintance drew her and Robert into a shared conversation. When their friend excused himself, Robert and Julie barely noticed. A spark of interest ignited.

"I was far gone within a week," Julie admitted.

As a bachelor in his mid-30s, Robert told Julie he had never married because he believed marriage was for a lifetime and that he had never met a person he desired to spend the rest of his life with.

"The value he placed on commitment touched me as nothing else could have. I had been married to a man that placed no worth on honest and real commitment."

Robert and Julie were engaged within three and a half months and married the following year. Because Robert had been visiting from out of town, their relationship spanned 120 miles. The distance made it easier for him to hide his alcoholism.

"Robert accepted Christ in his late teen years, but because of his addiction, he never grew," Julie said. "I was naive and didn't recognize the symptoms until much later. I thought alcoholics lived in gutters, but many are functioning and holding down jobs, living life like the rest of us."

The early years of their marriage were good, though neither was in a great place with God. Robert was drinking, and Julie hadn't completely healed from the wounds left by her previous husband. "I was weighed down by the cares of this world," she confessed.

"We didn't attend church regularly. I mostly did TV church. I used the excuse that I wanted Robert and me to choose a church together, but looking back, I avoided going since I wasn't living as I should. I didn't want to be around other Christians, because their lives illuminated my poor choices."

Robert nearly died and ended up in the hospital, forcing Julie to face the reality that she had married a man who drank too much. The good news was that God used her relationship with Robert to drive her to the foot of the Cross. He also used it to free her from being a control freak; no one can control an addict.

As Julie shared her story with me, I couldn't help thinking of the message of a song my son's high school choir used to sing: "When you discover Jesus is all you have, you'll realize He's all you need." In each of our lives, God will do what He must to bring us to the end of ourselves, and it's there we find Him and all the riches He has to offer.

At the end of herself, Julie called a man from the church she had previously attended. He was a good counselor and a recovering alcoholic. This man came alongside Robert and Julie and walked with them through this valley. He invited them to join a small group meeting in his home, and they began attending church regularly. This was a profound turning point for Julie.

"I knew I was home, I was back where I belonged, and God started doing a major work in my life. However, Robert wasn't there yet. He struggled and ended up in the hospital more than once." For the next eight years, his battle drained them emotionally and financially.

The cry of my heart, and I believe the cry of every woman's heart, is for her husband to be the spiritual leader of their home.

"The cry of my heart, and I believe the cry of every woman's heart, is for her husband to be the spiritual leader of their home. As I let go of things that I previously had tried to control, I sought the Lord in more and more ways. I was hungry for God, and as I fed on His Word, the Lord changed me. Robert quietly observed the transformation. I quit playing Holy Spirit in Robert's life, and the more I backed off, the more room God had to work.

"Just a little over a year ago, he had a major alcoholic meltdown. I went into a tailspin, not knowing what to do anymore. There wasn't anything to do except totally trust. I despaired that my marriage couldn't be saved, but the Lord spoke to me from the Book of Malachi: "'I hate divorce,' says the LORD God of Israel' (2:16). I immediately knew in my heart that this was God's promise to save my marriage.

"I gave it all over to Him and have seen a miracle in the past several months. I'm living with a walking miracle. I've watched Robert surrender to the Lord and stop drinking, and he's even reading the Word! The Word is where we grow; we have to be feeding on it. That is what has made the difference for Robert this time. Though he met

Christ nearly 30 years ago, he has finally returned to Him and has surrendered, making Him Lord of his life.

"Despite all we had been through, we never lost our commitment to one another, and we never lost sight of the fact that God put us together. We wanted our marriage to work. Now my husband not only attends church with me but also sings on the worship team!"

LESSONS FROM JULIE

I asked Julie what hope and encouragement she could provide for women in similar situations. Here's the wisdom she shared:

- Chase and seek God.
- Be obedient to His Word first.
- Fall in love with the Lord more deeply each day.
- Quit asking God to change your spouse, and ask Him to change you.
- Remember: it's not about you—it's about Jesus.
- Get your eyes off yourself and focused on Him.
- Accept God's forgiveness, and forgive yourself.
- Get into a small group of believers that affords accountability.
- Be sensitive, and don't cause your husband to feel he is less than you.
- Let him see a life of obedience—no words necessary.

"Seek Jesus' face," Julie said. "The more I pursue God, the more He will change me. Life isn't about everything being hunky-dory, but about what I can do for the Lord. How can I live right for Him today, and how can I serve Him more effectively? As I concentrate on these things, then God is free to work as He pleases.

"He prepares us and gives us all the tools we'll need for whatever we must face. He knows we're fragile. One of the lessons I learned over the years is that nothing touches my life that isn't filtered through the hands of a loving

Father. So whatever crisis is occurring, if I understand that, I can hang on and stand firm. Bad things happen because I live in a fallen world or because I've made bad choices. But whatever the reason, grasping the truth that God is in control—no matter how out of control my life feels—makes all the difference."

LESSONS FROM OTHERS

David, Ellen's husband, is also an alcoholic. He, however, makes no claim to Christ. Ellen spent years living the lie with David, pretending everything was wonderful when inside she was dying a thousand deaths. His drinking contributed to aggressive behavior, including emotional abuse. When drunk, he would become angry and accusatory.

Ellen distanced herself from relatives and was careful not to let friends get too close. She kept up a facade, painting a picture of a perfect world that didn't exist.

"Hiding an addiction only adds fuel to the flame. Covering for David, lying for him, and excusing his behavior only made the situation worse."

Julie, on the other hand, admits to what she says is probably too much sharing with too many people on a couple of occasions. "I'm a pretty up-front, here-I-am, tell-the-whole-truth-to-everybody kind of person. I learned to be spiritually discerning and discreet, but I also needed support and people praying for me as the wife of a practicing alcoholic. I sought prayer support from trusted individuals but didn't announce to the world my husband's plight."

So from these two very different women I learned that dealing with addictive behaviors, as with everything else in life, requires balance in what's said and how much is said to whom. There's a narrow line between telling your story and not finding support for yourself.

If your spouse is struggling with any kind of addiction, heed Julie's advice. She found the peace that passes all understanding even before Robert surrendered. In Julie's testimony, I see evidence of Rom. 8:28—"We know that in all things God works for the good of those who love him, who have been called according to his purpose." God redeems hard situations and brings good from them. He did it for Julie, He has done it for me, and He'll do it for you.

LESSONS FROM SCRIPTURE

Let's look at two men—one who started poorly but ended well and another who started well but ended poorly. First let's look at Samson, one of the judges. Set apart at birth as a Nazarite, he was dedicated to the Lord for His service, yet he disregarded the Nazarite vows. He maintained evil associations and possessed carnal appetites. Though mighty in physical strength, he displayed weakness in areas of temptation, especially the temptation of Delilah.

Samson spent most of his life doing his own thing. He fell in love with Delilah, but she conspired with the enemy to discover the root of his strength. Her ultimate goal was to ascertain the secret of his strength and reveal it to the Philistines so they could overpower him.

Many times she asked, but he always lied. Finally, growing sick of her constant badgering, he admitted his might was a result of his hair never having been cut. Then she lulled him to sleep and called a man to cut off his seven braids. Both his strength and the Lord left him.

The Philistines came upon him and gouged out his eyes. Then they set him to grinding in the prison. Later they brought him out of prison to entertain them in their temple.

Samson said to the servant who held his hand, "Put me where I can feel the pillars that support the temple, so that I may lean against them." Now the temple was crowded with men and women . . . watching Samson perform. Then Samson prayed to the LORD, "O Sovereign LORD, remember me. O God, please strengthen me just once more, and let me with one blow get revenge on the Philistines for my two eyes." Then Samson reached toward the two central pillars on which the temple stood. Bracing himself against them, his right hand on the one and his left hand on the other, Samson said, "Let me die with the Philistines!" Then he pushed with all his might, and down came the temple on the rulers and all the people in it. Thus he killed many more when he died than while he lived *(Judg. 16:26-30).*

The Lord allowed Samson one last victory, probably his most profound, because for once he called on God for help. Samson had every opportunity to win the race from start to finish, but he didn't actually start his race with the Lord at his side until the very end of his life.

The story of Judas is quite different. One of the 12 disciples, Judas spent a lot of time in the presence of Jesus. Outwardly, he looked good. Yet in the end he sold out for 30 pieces of silver and betrayed Christ with a kiss. He regretted his decision and ended up hanging himself—a tragic end to what looked like a promising start.

Remember: it's not how you start but how you finish that counts. I want my whole race to be one of surrender. I don't want to live a self-absorbed life like Samson's and hope for a strong finish. I also don't desire everything to look good on the outside while the inside is crumbling away.

PONDERING GOD'S WORD

- "'My food,' said Jesus, 'is to do the will of him who sent me and to finish his work'" (John 4:34).

- "I consider my life worth nothing to me, if only I may finish the race and complete the task the Lord Jesus has given me" (Acts 20:24).
- "Now finish the work, so that your eager willingness to do it may be matched by your completion of it, according to your means" (2 Cor. 8:11).
- "Ah, Sovereign LORD, you have made the heavens and the earth by your great power and outstretched arm. Nothing is too hard for you" (Jer. 32:17).
- "See, the Sovereign LORD comes with power" (Isa. 40:10).

Sovereign Lord,

I'm so grateful You're in control and that I don't have to be. Forgive me for the times I forget this truth and try to run the show myself. Help me remember when life is hard that whatever I'm dealing with has passed through Your loving hand, and whatever You've allowed to touch my life is for my greater good and Your greater glory.

Lord, even though my husband doesn't struggle with addictions, remind me to chase and seek You, to be obedient to Your Word, and enable me to fall in love with You more deeply each day. I promise to quit asking You to change Dean, but instead I'll plead, "Change me." May I remember that this life isn't about me—it's about You, so I must get my eyes off myself and focus on You alone.

Teach me to accept Your forgiveness and to forgive myself. May I not make my husband feel less than me. My heart's desire is that he see a life of obedience—without words. And for women who don't have believing husbands, provide them with a small group of believers that affords accountability. It's for the glory of Your name I pray. Amen.

Listening to God's Voice

What attitudes or actions in your life might God want to change?

_____

_____

_____

_____

_____

_____

_____

_____

_____

_____

_____

_____

_____

4

My Wistful Heart
Cultivating a Healthy Thought Life

From my pew near the back of the crowded sanctuary, my gaze roamed from family to family. A couple toward the front snuggled close together, and a pang of longing filled me. Another husband draped his arm around his wife's shoulders and drew her against his side. The pastor's words rang forth in bold proclamation, but my mind tuned him out as I focused on my own pain and misery.

Perched on every pew were happy, loving couples. Every man had a wife. Every woman had a husband—every woman except me. The ache in my heart increased in intensity. I felt lonelier at church than at any other place on earth. I yearned for the most important person in my world to be seated beside me, but he chose to stay home.

If only he had come. In my mind's eye, I envisioned us nestled together in a pew, sharing a Bible, taking turns flipping to the appropriate verses. He, of course, would know the Scriptures better than I and could find even the tiny, obscure Old Testament books in a matter of seconds. He would glance at me with adoration in his eyes, and I would smile up at him with such pride.

All right—I'm a bit of a sap, a dreamer, overly romantic. Skip the adoring glances; I would settle for a simple pew partner—if he would just come to church.

Continually I imagined, hoped, and dreamed what my life might be like once Dean accepted Christ. The harder I wished, the more discontented I became. Living in the land of "if-only" was a dangerous place to reside and made the land of reality hard to abide. I now avoid wishful thinking—nothing positive or productive happens there. Instead, I focus on accepting my spouse and not lingering in the "Please, oh, please believe!" stage.

Learning this lesson has decreased the tension in our marriage. Dean resented my gentle prodding, subtle hints, and the occasional hit over his head with a frying pan full of my expectations. I now aim for harmony between us by accepting him where he is—no more "if-onlys."

How do I avoid them? I do so by prayerfully retraining my brain to take captive my thoughts. I choose to appreciate my hubby, thanking God every day for him, our relationship, and his many wonderful attributes. This approach has made a world of difference in my marriage and in me.

I'm attempting to see the cup half full rather than half empty. The truth is, even happy, loving couples have their own problems. Having a Christian husband isn't the answer to all life's troubles. I must keep a truthful perspective.

I pray faithfully for God to draw Dean to himself, but until that occurs, I need to concentrate on the work God wants to do in me. And believe me: there's a lot to ponder. God's concern is my character. He desires me to be focused on Him, not my circumstances.

Several years ago I attended a seminar on prayer. The speaker talked about our gaze and our glance. If our gaze is on God, then our circumstances are bearable, but when we only glance at God while gazing at life, living overwhelms us. I'm working at keeping my gaze on God alone, and when I do, those are the peace-filled, joy-filled, life's-not-so-bad times.

Look at Peter—when his gaze rested on Jesus, he walked on water. The minute he lowered his eyes to the waves, he sank. I want to walk through this life with my eyes on Christ, because otherwise I too easily sink into overwhelming discouragement.

CONSIDER YOUR SPOUSE'S POINT OF VIEW

All along I thought I was the only frustrated partner in this relationship, but a conversation with a friend at lunch and then with God revealed otherwise.

"He just doesn't 'get' you anymore," Darlene said. Her expression mirrored her uncertainty as to how much she should reveal.

I stirred my iced tea in frustration. "What's not to 'get'?" I asked, hearing a defensive tone rise in my voice. I glanced around the restaurant filled with patrons. "He's the one being difficult, refusing to change."

"And you're the one who *has* changed. Dean told Dennis he hardly recognizes his own wife anymore. Think about it, Jeri. You're different—no longer the girl he married. And on top of that, he says you seem angry all the time because he's not joining you in this new religious kick."

Truth smacked me between the eyes. On the drive home, I poured out my heart to God. I saw reality clearly for the first time. God enabled me to see my poor husband's plight. He had married one girl and now found himself saddled with another. Sure enough, I had become a new creation in Christ. He had begun a radical transformation in my life, leaving Dean married to a

God enabled me to see my poor husband's plight. He had married one girl and now found himself saddled with another. Sure enough, I had become a new creation in Christ.

stranger—an angry stranger who wanted him to be just like her.

Growth in Christ changes views, lifestyles, and people. As my friend Kathy once commented: "As my walk with God expanded, my husband liked me less and less, though I know he still loved me." No surprise there; after all, the apostle Paul asked, "What fellowship can light have with darkness?" (2 Cor. 6:14). Sometimes the differences seem huge, both to our spouses and to us.

Your spouse, like mine, may occasionally wonder where this fanatic kook or Jesus freak came from. He may share the same sentiment Peter did, certain that we are indeed "a peculiar people" (1 Pet. 2:9, KJV).

When Jill came to Christ, Rob shared that he felt replaced by someone he couldn't see, hear, or understand. He admitted to bouts of jealousy and feeling unimportant and unacceptable. Why? Because he sensed his wife longed to change him and knew she had strangers praying for him. Jill had new friends he had never met, suddenly listened to weird music, and no longer approved of his movie choices. She spoke a new language he barely understood and attended church as if her life depended on it. Not only that—she wanted him to go too!

Seeing another perspective helped me realize that an unequally yoked marriage is a tough trek on either side of the street. When I think the walking is hard in my shoes, maybe I need to slip into Dean's boots and try a mile or two in them. I'm discovering that life with me is no stroll in the park.

AVOID THE COMPARISON TRAP

I'm convinced that the grass always looks greener on the other side of the fence. The truth is that if I search long and hard enough, I'll run upon a man who appears better than the one I have. Flip the coin, and I can find a guy who doesn't measure up. But what I think I see and the truth of what happens inside a family can be two very different things.

Years ago, Dean and I spent lots of time with Lee and Allie. Allie boasted continuously about her perfect husband. "Lee would never do that." "Lee always says that." "I wouldn't be able to stand Lee speaking to me in that tone of voice." "I don't know how you put up with him. You're much more patient and accepting than I would be."

After a few years of Allie's constant comparisons, I didn't know how I survived either. I found myself depressed, because in her eyes my husband didn't make the grade. Soon he wasn't good enough in my opinion either. I wondered why he couldn't be more like Lee. Why did he do things and say things Lee never would? Lee must love Allie more than Dean loved me.

Though we enjoyed our friendship with Lee and Allie, eventually we had to pull back and lessen contact. The subtle contrasting eroded my opinion of my husband, and slowly, over time, discontentment grew in my heart like weeds overtaking a garden. I realized that no matter how much fun we had together, the pleasure didn't outweigh the subsequent pain. I would go home after an evening out with them and cry myself to sleep. The damage to my marriage wasn't worth the pleasure of their company.

Through this ordeal, God taught me that each of us is wonderfully made and woven together by the Master Craftsman. Dean isn't Lee and never will be, but Lee isn't Dean either.

On the other hand, I've been guilty of a little comparison-shopping myself. I can build my guy up if I find someone I think is lesser, but do I really want to make someone think of her husband the way Allie caused me to think of mine? Do I desire to cause pain to someone else just to make myself feel better about my situation? Paul reminded each person to "test his own actions. Then he can take pride in himself, without comparing himself to somebody else" (Gal. 6:4).

My marriage won't resemble anyone else's, because my husband and I are unique individuals, created by God, and there aren't two more like us anywhere on the face of this earth.

My marriage won't resemble anyone else's, because my husband and I are unique individuals, created by God, and there aren't two more like us anywhere on the face of this earth. And, yes, someone else's relationship with her husband may resemble my dream come true, but I keep reminding myself that what you see isn't always what you get. No one but God truly knows what goes on behind closed doors.

I learned this lesson firsthand not long ago. An acquaintance I've known for almost 20 years recently revealed physical and emotional abuse in her marriage. I would never have guessed, and actually I would have placed them on my top-10 list of happy couples with successful marriages and functional families. But the picture they presented to the world was only a facade. Many women who traveled in our circle envied Darcy, wishing they had what she did with Steve. Now with the truth exposed, we're all grateful for the guys we have. Steve suddenly lost his appeal.

IN SUMMARY

Everything I've discussed thus far ties into one thing—my thought life. If I'm to avoid wishful thinking and comparisons, I must take control of my thought patterns.

Even understanding how my husband feels results from having compassionate thoughts about the hardships he faces in our unequally yoked relationship.

Let's look at two examples from Scripture: one man took control of his thoughts, and one did not. First consider Job. After his first test when some of his livestock was stolen and the rest destroyed, and his servants, sons, and daughters were killed, Job did not sin or charge God with wrongdoing. In chapter 1, verse 21, he said, "Naked I came from my mother's womb, and naked I will depart. The LORD gave and the LORD has taken away; may the name of the LORD be praised."

In his second test, God allowed Satan to afflict Job with painful sores from the top of his head to the soles of his feet. "His wife said to him, 'Are you still holding on to your integrity? Curse God and die!' He replied, 'You are talking like a foolish woman. Shall we accept good from God, and not trouble?' In all this, Job did not sin in what he said" (2:9-10).

This is a man who controlled his thoughts. How do I know? Because Jesus said, "The things that come out of the mouth come from the heart, and these make a man 'unclean.' For out of the heart come evil thoughts" (Matt. 15:18-19). What we think about infiltrates our heart and spews out of our mouths.

What poured forth from Job's mouth? Only words honoring God. Check out these examples: "His wisdom is profound, his power is vast" (9:4). "I know that my Redeemer lives, and that in the end he will stand upon the earth" (19:25). "He knows the way that I take; when he has tested me, I will come forth as gold" (23:10).

Job stated my heart's desire—to come forth as gold. This was true for him because he prohibited displeasing thoughts from controlling him. In the end the Lord gave him twice as much as he had before. Blessing follows obedience.

Now let's contrast Job with the story of David. David is called a man after God's own heart, but with Bathsheba, David let his thoughts carry him into sin. When he looked at her, he failed to turn away. As stated in James, "But each one is tempted when, by his own evil desire, he is dragged away and enticed. Then, after desire has conceived, it gives birth to sin; and sin, when it is full-grown, gives birth to death" (1:14-15).

James paints a clear picture of what happened to David. Maybe David felt restless. He rose from his bed and took an evening stroll around the palace roof. Who knows what thoughts were rumbling through his mind? Perhaps he was simply enjoying the newness and excitement that spring brings.

Then he saw her. His eyes must have lingered on the bathing woman long enough for him to take note of her beauty, long enough to realize he wanted to know more about her. Instead of turning and fleeing, he let his own evil desire drag him away and entice him. Then he sent someone to find out who she was.

David learned her name, her father's name, and her husband's name. The information should have been enough to send him packing, but he had obviously been thinking about her, lusting after her. His desire had been conceived, and with his next decision—to send for her— desire gave birth to sin.

When she arrived, David took her to his bed. Then she went back home. I'm assuming he had planned for her to be a one-night stand—until she sent word that she was carrying his child. In a last-ditch effort, he brought her husband, Uriah, home from war, hoping he would enjoy his wife's company and assume the baby belonged to him.

David's plan failed when Uriah slept at the city gate rather than going home to Bathsheba. Can you see how David tried to cover his own tracks by scheming and manipulating, which involved more thoughts run amuck? Uriah never cooperated, and David's sin ultimately led to two deaths.

First, he had Uriah placed on the front lines, and the troops behind him retreated. Sure, he looked like a casualty of war, but in truth David arranged his death. Later the son Bathsheba conceived in adultery also died.

Worse yet, "This is what the LORD says: 'Out of your own household I am going to bring calamity upon you. Before your very eyes I will take your wives and give them to one who is close to you, and he will lie with your wives in broad daylight. You did it in secret, but I will do this thing in broad daylight before all Israel'" (2 Sam. 12:11-12).

The contrast is startling. God blessed Job twofold, and David's life changed forever in the other direction. And both stories began with a thought. That's enough to make me rethink my thinking. I want God's blessing, not calamity.

PONDERING GOD'S WORD

- "An upright [woman] gives thought to [her] ways" (Prov. 21:29).
- "As [she] thinks within [herself] so [she] is" (Prov. 23:7, NASB).
- "The mind controlled by the Spirit is life and peace" (Rom. 8:6).
- "We take captive every thought to make it obedient to Christ" (2 Cor. 10:5).
- "Whatever is true, whatever is noble, whatever is right, whatever is pure, whatever is lovely, whatever is admirable—if anything is excellent or praiseworthy—think about such things" (Phil. 4:8).

Father God,

Teach me to take captive my thoughts. May I be an upright woman who gives thought to my ways—especially the ways I think about my spouse. Remind me to have thoughts pleasing to You, so that I will be pleasing to You. I pray for a mind controlled by the Holy Spirit and a life filled with peace. Teach me to focus my thoughts on things true, noble, right, pure, lovely, admirable, excellent, and praiseworthy.

Thank You for my spouse. Forgive me for the times I've been discontent, demanding, and discouraged. Teach me to be grateful and appreciative of the man I'm yoked to. Thank You for my husband and his many wonderful qualities. Teach me to be a blessing in his life. And, Lord, continually draw him to You.

I'm so grateful for Your faithfulness. May my gaze be on You and You alone. To Your name be the glory both now and forevermore. I love You, Lord. I pray in the righteous, holy, worthy name of Jesus Christ. Amen.

Listening to God's Voice

Ask God to help you see your husband through His eyes.
Record your impressions below.

_____

_____

_____

_____

_____

_____

_____

_____

_____

_____

_____

_____

_____

_____

_____

5
My Amigas and Me
Friendships Are Vital

A few months after my commitment to follow the high road to spiritual growth, our marriage hit a huge pothole. I wasn't sure we would survive the crisis. The problem wasn't a result of my Christian growth but perhaps a diversion the enemy threw at me to distract me from that endeavor. The good news is that I sought God more, and even though I crossed one of the lowest valleys of my life, my sweet times with Him carried me through. But the sad news was I stood knee-deep in grief, sorrow, and pain, and not a living soul had a clue.

My previous friendships before I recommitted my life to Christ had fizzled. We didn't have much in common anymore, and they didn't care for the new, Christian version of me. I had made many acquaintances at church but had yet to establish a deep, sharing relationship. I had vowed long before not to drag relatives into my marital difficulties, so I faced life painfully alone and isolated when I desperately needed a friend's prayers, encouragement, and a shoulder to cry on.

We made the trek through the tough season, just God and I, but I realized I never wanted to be in that lonely, friendless place again. So I asked God for a Christian friend to walk beside me on this sometimes-hard road, someone who would share the tough times and understand my plight. I yearned for another person to share my prayers, hopes, and fears and to understand all the vicissitudes of my spiritual journey. I wished for an intimate friend, a transparent friend.

God, I asked each day, *please bring someone into my life to share this load.*

A couple of weeks later I met Kathy. We were assigned to coteach a Sunday School class for five-year-olds. Her husband also stayed home from church, and they had four children close in age to my three. We shared similar concerns in the spiritual matters of our children's lives and identified with one another's longings and loneliness. Eighteen years have now passed, and I still thank God for the blessing of our friendship.

We never know when He'll answer or exactly how, but He will answer.

If you don't have a friend like Kathy in your life, I encourage you to ask God to provide one. Remember—His timetable is often different for each of us, and seldom does He work on our schedule.

My friend Sandy heard a woman speak about friendship on a radio broadcast more than 15 years ago. Sandy had recently quit her job to stay at home with her firstborn and longed for a godly friend. Accepting the speaker's challenge, Sandy began to pray for a special friend too.

God didn't answer Sandy's prayer as quickly as she would have liked. In faith she believed God would provide a friend; she just didn't know when. When Sandy finally met Laura, she said to God, "I know this can't be her!" But she was the answer to Sandy's prayer. The two have been dear friends for 12 years. We never know when He'll answer or exactly how, but He *will* answer. His answers don't always look like our expectations, but He knows best. Now she wouldn't trade Laura for the world.

SOLOMON WAS RIGHT

"Two are better than one, because they have a good return for their work: If one falls down, his friend can help him up. But pity the man who falls and has no one to help him up!" (Eccles. 4:9-10). Kathy and I encouraged one another through hard situations and prodigal periods in our children's lives. Leaning on her got me through my mother-in-law's cancer, and I supported her a few months later when she became a widow with four teenagers to finish raising.

I found tremendous relief over the years in sharing my burdens with my dear friend. We frequently sat together in church and attended church training classes together. I was comforted knowing Kathy would be there, and I wouldn't have to face everything alone. We've laughed together, we've cried together, and we've occasionally called the other to task.

Friendship is about honesty and caring. Christian friendship is about accountability, spurring one another on toward love and good deeds and asking each other the hard questions. Kathy and I have done those things; we've shared the difficult lessons God is teaching us and have prayed faithfully for each other. Along with Solomon, I feel for the woman who has no one to reach down and help her up should she stumble and fall and the woman who has never known the joy of a close friendship.

Friendship is a gift from the Lord and important to everyone but especially so for an unequally yoked woman. If we can't share our Christian experiences with our spouses, we need someone we can share with and someone to hold us accountable to God's Word. We need a godly friend with whom to communicate our spiritual concerns and someone to occasionally shoulder the weight of our distress.

PRAYER PARTNERS

I often felt so alone in my mothering, knowing my kids didn't have a father who prayed for them or worried about their spiritual well-being. I dared not miss a day of praying, because if I did, who would take up the slack? Sometimes the enormous responsibility overwhelmed me.

One Sunday my pastor preached a sermon on raising godly offspring. The statistics he quoted for children from one-parent spiritual households growing up to be godly were bleak—only one in four lived for the Lord after reaching adulthood. What chance did I have for my three children? My heart ached to beat those odds.

I discovered that Kathy and another friend from Bible study, Val, shouldered the same concerns. Though Val wasn't unequally yoked, the three of us committed to meet together and pray for our families. For nearly a decade, we reserved Monday nights for a time of eating, sharing, and praying. I confess that we subscribed to the theory that good Christians couldn't meet together without breaking a little bread.

We all need people who love us enough to confront us.

Those times were precious times, and we celebrated God's awesome answers. We prayed kids through dating relationships, adjustments from Christian school to public school, surgery, broken hearts, skinned elbows, marriage proposals, the loss of a father, home schooling choices, and most other imaginable kid problems.

Knowing these two dear Christian women prayed for my kids on a daily basis and approached God with the same dedication they did for their own children meant the world to me. My burden lightened, and as I prayed for their families, I grew to love their kids with a deep, abiding love.

Another blessing is the accountability other members of a group provide. These friends kept me on my toes spiritually, because I knew they would ask the tough questions. We all need people who love us enough to confront us. If you don't have a prayer partner in your life, prayerfully seek one. Though my relationships with Kathy and Val have changed and we no longer pray together every week, I still love them and pray *for* them.

Most things in life are only for a season. I'd like everything to stay the same forever, but it rarely does.

God has faithfully provided different praying friends for the current season in my life. Monica and I pray for the needs of our adult children, and Sandy and I challenge each other in our faith walk, praying for our families, our church, and our friends. But mostly we pray for one another to be Christlike.

IN SUMMARY

Friends are an important part of life and have a dramatic influence on us. God gave Jesus 12 companions, and of those 12, 3 became intimate friends. As women, we need intimate friends because, as James Dobson has pointed out, men aren't equipped to meet all our emotional needs.

You've probably heard the old adage "To have a friend, you must be one." Proverbs instructs us in the qualities of a good friend. Solomon says these characteristics should be evident in me. I should be faithful, honest, wise, loving, slow to anger, humble, and have integrity. What a challenge!

Now let's look to God's Word for an example of godly friendship contrasted with a man abandoned by his friends. God gave David an incredible friend in Jonathan.

"Jonathan made a covenant with David because he loved him as himself" (1 Sam. 18:3). Then Jonathan removed his robe, tunic, sword, bow, and even his belt, handing them to David. By removing his royal regalia, the robe and tunic, and giving them to David, Jonathan symbolically acknowledged David as Israel's next king. Jonathan was King Saul's son and technically next in line for the throne, but God had already anointed David for the job. Many of us would have been in there fighting for our birthright, but Jonathan willingly gave it up.

Later Saul planned to kill David, but Jonathan spoke on David's behalf. Saul listened and agreed to spare him. A prime opportunity presented itself for Jonathan to get David out of his way and reclaim his future on the throne of Israel, but he not only loved David but defended him as well.

Saul's agreement to spare David lasted only a short while, but his renewed threat of death upon David only created a stronger bond of friendship between David and Jonathan. "Then they kissed each other and wept together—but David wept the most. Jonathan said to David, 'Go in peace, for we have sworn friendship with each other in the name of the LORD, saying, "The LORD is witness between you and me, and between your descendants and my descendants forever."' Then David left, and Jonathan went back to town" (1 Sam. 20:41-42).

When Jonathan died in battle, David tore his clothes and grieved. In his lament he said, "I grieve for you, Jonathan my brother; you were very dear to me. Your love for me was wonderful, more wonderful than that of women" (2 Sam. 1:26). I not only want a friend like him but also desire to be that kind of friend.

David also went through a time in his life when he felt abandoned and friendless. In Ps. 38:11 he wrote, "My friends and my companions avoid me because of my wounds; my neighbors stay far away." In another psalm he says, "Because of all my enemies, I am the utter contempt of my neighbors; I am a dread to my friends—those who see me on the street flee from me. I am forgotten by them as though I were dead" (31:11-12). I wonder if he longed for Jonathan in those times.

Even Jesus—though He had nine companions and His three amigos—experienced times of complete abandonment. Let's look at the night of the Last Supper. He spent the evening with His disciples, they shared a meal, and He washed their feet. He knew His time on earth was coming to a close and probably wished that just once He could count on this group of men, but they seemed to let Him down often.

After the meal, He led them to a place called Gethsemane. He told the nine to sit and wait while He escorted Peter, James, and John farther. He spoke of deep sorrow and asked them to stay and keep watch while He went on farther still. After spending some time in prayer, He returned to find them asleep. He left them a second time and then a third, finding them sleeping each time He returned.

Judas, Christ's betrayer, approached, and Jesus was arrested. The remaining disciples deserted Him and fled (Mark 14:50). As if the situation weren't bad enough, Peter, one of the three from His inner circle, denied knowing Him three times.

Jesus knows what it's like to have no one there for you. He knows how you feel when those you count on jump ship. If you ever find yourself in such a place, count on the fact that His love can get you through.

PONDERING GOD'S WORD

- "A friend loves at all times" (Prov. 17:17).

- "As iron sharpens iron, so one [woman] sharpens another" (Prov. 27:17).
- "Two are better than one, because they have a good return for their work: If one falls down, [her] friend can help [her] up. But pity the [woman] who falls and has no one to help [her] up!" (Eccles. 4:9-10).
- "Greater love has no one than this, that [she] lay down [her] life for [her] friends" (John 15:13).
- "I no longer call you servants, because a servant does not know [her] master's business. Instead, I have called you friends, for everything I have learned from my Father I have made known to you" (John 15:15).

Father God,

Teach me to be a better friend, a Jonathan. I still have much to learn and many areas in which I need to grow. Most important, though, enable me to be a good friend to my husband, to encourage him and appreciate him. I pray we would be the best of friends. Remind me to treat him the way Your Son treated His friends.

I thank You for the treasured friends You've brought into my life—people to sit in church with, to pray with, and to encourage me. I even thank You for the times of friendlessness, that through those days I have learned the true value of having and being a friend. Friendship and friends are a gift from Your hand. May I never take them for granted.

I'm so grateful for You in my life. You are my most faithful and dearest friend of all. I love You, Lord. I pray in the strong name of Jesus. Amen.

Listening to God's Voice

Write a prayer for your best friend.

_____

_____

_____

_____

_____

_____

_____

_____

_____

_____

_____

_____

_____

_____

_____

6

Avoiding Forbidden Fruit
Fleeing from Temptation

"Maybe I'll stop by tomorrow. I know your evenings get long and lonely when Jake's at work." Chris paused at Lisa's front door. He slowly turned to face her. Their eyes locked, and instinctively she knew he wanted to kiss her. What frightened her more than the prospect of his kiss was the fact that she, too, wanted it, longed for it, even dreamed of it.

In the next heart-stopping moment, Chris swept her into his arms, kissing her with a passion she hadn't experienced in years. Her lips, of their own accord, returned his kiss. Her mind screamed no, but her heart cried yes. This was Chris—her husband's good friend. What was she doing?

Moments later Lisa heard Chris whisper, "I think I'm falling in love with you. I don't know what to do—you're Jake's wife." His guilt-filled blue eyes begged for forgiveness and understanding.

Lisa didn't know what to do either. She stood face-to-face with temptation: not a piece of fruit but a hunk of muscle with inviting eyes, eyes that held a promise of forbidden pleasure. He gently laid his warm hand against her cheek. "I want you—I need you," his pain-filled voice whispered. With awe, his lips found hers again.

What about Jake? Lisa didn't want to remember. She longed to continue along this path of discovery, reveling in the emotions this man evoked in her. She teetered on the brink of a tawdry affair that would destroy a friendship and a marriage. Lisa hung motionless between right and wrong.

"Stop!" she exclaimed, backing out of Chris's embrace. "I can't do this." Hurt and rejection etched themselves across his face. "I feel the same way you do, but I've never been with anyone but Jake. I made a vow to him. No matter how much I would like to, I can't. I just can't." Tears rolled down her cheeks.

Why was she so vulnerable to another man when she loved her husband?

"I'm sorry," Chris responded. "I never intended to hurt you." He wiped a tear away with gentle fingers. "I can't come back anymore."

"I know," Lisa whispered through the lump in her throat. As Chris left, the closing of the door brought a finality that made the ache in her heart increase. She crumpled in a heap on the floor, wondering why right choices often felt wrong at the time, and wrong choices felt so right.

Over the next few days, Lisa wondered how this had happened. Why was she so vulnerable to another man when she loved her husband? As she thought back over her relationships with Jake and with Chris, she made some important discoveries.

VULNERABILITIES EXPOSED

Chris gave Lisa the gift of time. She felt lonesome for companionship. Jake worked long hours, often late into the night. When home, he busied himself with his hobbies and interests. Lisa longed for someone to pay attention to her. She wanted to feel important, needed, and valued.

Chris affirmed her as a person of worth by investing himself in her. Jake found time for her only in their bedroom. Loneliness left her vulnerable to anyone willing to shower her with attention.

Chris talked to Lisa, and more important, he listened. When he dropped by, he focused on her, not the television, the newspaper, or the computer. He shared the little things in his life and later revealed some of his hopes and dreams for the future.

They became good friends. Conversation flowed freely. He listened when she talked, even asking questions. He laughed at her jokes, believed in her dreams, and encouraged her to converse for hours. Jake missed half of what she said because his mind was elsewhere. Chris valued Lisa as a human being, cared about her opinions, and respected her intelligence. Conversation with Jake dried up within their first year of marriage, not because she didn't long for it, but because he showed no interest.

Chris told Lisa things a woman likes and needs to hear. He often complimented her cooking, her outfit, or her thoughts on an issue. On that fateful night, he spoke the words she had longed to hear Jake say for years—he needed and wanted her. Lisa, a neglected housewife, felt irresistible for the first time in years. The problem was that the wrong man evoked those feelings.

Chris's thoughtful considerations shined through all his interactions with Lisa. Little things seem to matter the most. Just as the proverbial one straw broke the camel's back, the tiny courtesies shown in daily living carry the most weight. Chris looked at Lisa when they talked, walked beside her instead of leaving her eating his dust, and cared when she felt upset or down.

Chris treated Lisa with a tender reverence. He kissed her with an awe that Jake lost long ago. He showed her respect and treasured her. His actions reflected how much she mattered to him.

As all women through the ages, Lisa yearned to feel attractive and desired by her husband. Instead, she felt unimportant, lonely, and vulnerable. Lisa had not planned or sought after anyone else, but the opportunity landed in her lap. In her weakness, she found the temptation almost more than she could bear.

IN SUMMARY

As I've interviewed and talked with countless Christian women across the country, I've run into many Lisas. Some have had adulterous relationships, seeking to fill a void in their lives. Others have contemplated an affair or committed emotional adultery. The sad truth is that when it's over, they're left with enormous guilt, shame, and grief. Sin is pleasurable for a season—the writer to the Hebrews assures us of that—but when the season ends, the heartbreak begins.

We can become entangled in an emotional affair in a couple of different ways.

We can become entangled in an emotional affair in a couple of different ways. As women, we need to guard against the forbidden fruit of temptation Satan may dangle before us. One type of emotional adultery is when a woman admires a man, possibly even a stranger, from afar and daydreams or fantasizes about a romantic or sexual encounter with him. Remember that Jesus said, "I tell you that anyone who looks at a woman lustfully has already committed adultery with her in his heart" (Matt. 5:28). We live in a world that tells us fantasy is OK, but we have a God who tells us it's not.

Another type of emotional affair starts with a friendship.

As the friendship blossoms and sharing takes place, emotional intimacy grows. Suddenly, like Lisa, we find ourselves thinking more about another man than our own husband. Lisa told me that when something happened in her life, either good or bad, she found herself anticipating sharing her news with Chris, not Jake. That's a dangerous place to be.

Many women may find the following statement disputable, but I'll stand firm on it nevertheless. *Once you're married, to have a male friend who is more than a casual acquaintance is allowing yourself to flirt with danger.* Almost every one of us is vulnerable at one time or another to the attention of a male who isn't our husband. Why put yourself and your marriage at risk? Another interesting fact I ascertained in my research for this book is that unequally yoked women are often even more susceptible to the attentions of a kind Christian man than her equally yoked counterpart. That's one more reason to be on guard.

Remember when you first fell in love with your husband. Everything was new, fresh, exciting. The years wipe away the intensity, and we're left with sameness and routine. With Chris, Lisa rediscovered the *ain't-it-great-to-be-alive* sensations. She considers it nothing but God's grace that she was able to stop before she actually allowed herself to follow the desires of her heart.

"With everything in me, I wanted Chris. But as we kissed, the reality of my kids growing up in a divorced family stopped me. I couldn't do it to them."

That night when Jake returned home, Lisa lay sobbing on their bed. "Honey, what's wrong?" His voice sounded frightened. He sat beside her brushing her hair back out of her face. "Are you hurt? Did someone die?"

Lisa shook her head, trying to talk between the sobbing and sniffing. She poured out the story, confessing her guilt and shame. "Can you ever forgive me?"

To her surprise, Jake gathered her into his arms, and they cried together. "I know I'm partly to blame," he confessed. Realizing what they almost lost brought a new value to their marriage.

Chris never visited Jake and Lisa's home again. Losing him as a friend was worth the price of salvaging their marriage, and the renewed relationship with Jake is now Lisa's most treasured friendship.

"I don't allow myself to get close to any man anymore. I avoid everything—except a polite hello—like a dreaded disease. I concentrate on keeping my affections on Jake."

A LOOK AT GOD'S WORD

Let's look at Joseph, a very wise man who hightailed it out of Dodge when sexual sin came his way. Remember—he was the guy his jealous brothers sold into slavery. Once he arrived in Egypt, Potiphar, a member of the personal staff of Pharaoh, purchased him. Pharaoh was the king of Egypt, and Potiphar was the captain of his palace guard, a pretty important guy.

Joseph served with diligence, and Potiphar not only noticed but also realized the Lord was with him, giving him success in everything he did. Naturally, Joseph became the favored servant, and before long Potiphar placed him in charge of all his household affairs.

According to the account in Gen. 39, Joseph was a handsome and well-built young man. Potiphar's wife took notice, began to desire him, and eventually invited him to her bed. Joseph refused. How could he betray a man who trusted him implicitly? Joseph said, "How then could I do such a wicked thing and sin against God?" (v. 9).

Potiphar's wife continued to pressure Joseph day after day, but he stood firm in his refusal, avoiding her as much as possible. I think it's important for us to notice Joseph didn't waver, and I believe, based on what we learned in the chapter on our thought life, he never allowed himself to entertain the possibility. It's much easier to stand firm when my mind is made up. Don't consider the what-ifs.

One day when he entered the house to fulfill his duties, the place was empty. Not a servant lingered anywhere. Mrs. Potiphar swept into the room, grabbed him by the cloak, and demanded, "Come to bed with me!" He slipped out of his cloak and ran! Isn't this a great picture of Paul's admonition to flee sexual immorality? I wonder how far Joseph ran before he figured it was safe to stop.

Now, Mrs. Potiphar, obviously a woman who didn't take rejection well, decided to make Joseph pay for not giving in to her whims. She made up a whopper about how Joseph had sought her out for sexual favors, leaving his cloak behind when she screamed for help. Doing the right thing came at tremendous cost. Joseph ended up in prison, but at least he stood clean and right before God.

Now, let's contrast Joseph's story with the adulterous woman in the New Testament. Picture Jesus, around dawn, in the Temple courts surrounded by a gathering crowd. He sits down to teach, but the teachers of the Law and the Pharisees interrupt. They've brought a woman who committed adultery and force her to stand before the group while they tell Jesus what she's done and how she deserves stoning. After all, she was caught in the very act, and according to the Law of Moses, they're commanded to stone such a woman. Then they asked Jesus, "What do you say?"

I love all Jesus' encounters with people, but this is one of my very favorites. He stoops down and writes something in the dust with His finger. There's been much speculation over the years as to what He was actually writing, but I wonder if He could have been making a list of all their sins. They continue questioning Him, and He rises, saying, "If any one of you is without sin, let him be the first to throw a stone at her" (John 8:7). Then He bends down and continues writing on the ground.

If you've committed either emotional or physical adultery, accept His words as a gift, a healing balm for your heart.

At His words, the crowd dissipates, the older men leaving first, and not one of those self-righteous hypocrites bends over to pick up the first stone. When it's just Jesus and the woman, He asks her, "Woman, where are they? Has no one condemned you?"

"No one, sir," she says. "Then neither do I condemn you," Jesus says. "Go now and leave your life of sin" (vv. 10-11).

Don't you love the tender, forgiving heart of our Lord Jesus Christ? If you've committed either emotional or physical adultery, accept His words as a gift, a healing balm for your heart. Then heed His advice—"Go now and leave your life of sin." It's not too late to accept God's grace and choose the life of Joseph. Lay down the past, cling to Him, and flee.

PONDERING GOD'S WORD

- "I made a covenant with my eyes not to look lustfully at a [man]" (Job 31:1).
- "Flee from sexual immorality. All other sins a [person] commits are outside [his or her] body, but [he or she] who sins sexually sins against [his or her] own body" (1 Cor. 6:18).
- "It is God's will that you should be sanctified: that you should avoid sexual immorality" (1 Thess. 4:3).

- "You shall not commit adultery" (Exod. 20:14).
- "If we confess our sins, he is faithful and just and will forgive us our sins and purify us from all unrigh-teousness" (1 John 1:9).

My most precious Heavenly Father,

As I read the tender account between Jesus and the adulterous woman, my heart swells with gratitude at Your tender mercy. I may not have committed the act, but I have certainly entertained thoughts I shouldn't have. From this day forward, I would like to stand unwavering—as Joseph did—not veering to the left or the right, but fleeing from all temptation.

And, Lord, may I not cast stones at others. May I always re-member—though we don't all struggle with the same temptation, we all struggle with some temptation, whether it be adultery, pride, self-righteousness, gossip, complaining, nagging, or anything else. May I not search for the splinter in my sister's eye when there could easily be a log in mine.

I pray that my life will bring You glory, that I will keep my thoughts and words pure and that I will flee from danger. It's in the merciful name of my Lord and Savior that I pray. Amen.

Listening to God's Voice

Ask God to show you some practical ways to avoid temptation. Write them below.

_____

_____

_____

_____

_____

_____

_____

_____

_____

_____

_____

_____

_____

_____

7

Moving Mountains and Mowing Down Molehills
Prayer—Key to Success

Excited, I drove toward the church to pick up our youngest, Adam, who was 12 at the time. I had missed him, but more than that, I enjoyed watching my kids when they returned from camp. I knew he'd be bubbling over about Jesus. I couldn't wait to hear how God had revealed himself to my junior higher.

After a quick hello hug, we dug through the piles of sleeping bags, suitcases, and backpacks to unearth Adam's belongings. I waited through long, meaningful good-byes with his friends, and then we headed for home.

"You know what I realized, Mom?" Adam started as soon as we had pulled onto the street.

"No, what, Honey?"

"I realized I'd be willing to die for Dad to know Jesus."

The air left my body in a whoosh. Shocked, I had no idea how to react. I blinked double-time to fight the onslaught of tears. I'm still not sure—even a decade later—how I responded or how I successfully completed the drive home. I don't remember how or why he came to this conclusion. All I do remember is begging God not to take my son from me.

Amazingly, I had been studying the life of Abraham. Just the morning before, I had contemplated Abraham's willingness to put his own son on the altar. I have to confess, I had never been as faithful and trustworthy as Abraham. Now I wondered if my deeply rooted fear, that one of my children might have to die for Dean to know Christ, was about to happen.

From almost the moment I recommitted my life to the Lord, I had expected some tragedy to befall one of my kids.

From almost the moment I recommitted my life to the Lord, I had expected some tragedy to befall one of my kids. After all, it had taken my dad's death for me to come around, so I assumed it would take an equal heartbreak for God to get Dean's attention.

Another family member lost a child in infancy, and God used that incident to draw the deceased baby's parents to himself. Many humans aren't bright enough to come to Him of their own accord. They have to hit bottom before looking up.

I feared that would be the case with Dean, and anticipating the cost terrified me. I had not prayed for his salvation in my early walk, too petrified to even consider it. Later I approached God with fear and trembling, asking Him to draw Dean to Christ. Then I spent nearly two decades dreading the price of the prayer.

About a year and a half ago, God revealed that fear and anxiety was a generational stronghold in my family. Through my study, I began to realize how much God loves me and that whatever He has in store for my life and my kids' lives, it's His very best. His ways are not my ways, but I now trust Him completely, come what may.

I'm happy to report nothing came of Adam's passionate declaration, but God gave him a willing heart to obey whatever the cost. I'm touched, knowing Adam loves his dad and cares about his eternal salvation, even to the point of making a personal sacrifice if God asks. Didn't Jesus say a friend would lay down his life for another?

Remember my friend Susan who recently lost her son, Brian, to leukemia? I struggled with how anything good could come from the death of a 24-year-old, but the Word says God's goals are our growth and His glory. At least seven people made decisions for Christ at Brian's funeral. Countless others were touched by his love for the Lord Jesus. Prodigals returned to the fold. Much was accomplished for the Kingdom. And now Brian, fully healed, is in heaven, revering a holy, righteous, and worthy God. May I never fail to trust Him, even when this life makes no sense.

Prayers for Hubby

Eventually I forced myself to start praying for Dean despite the fear. I wasn't sure how or what to request, so I asked, *Lord, teach me to pray for my husband.* I'm one of those organized types, a list maker for sure, and I needed a plan in order to tackle this new task the Lord had placed before me. From reading the Bible and talking to others, I made a list of the top 10 areas in my husband's life that I felt needed prayer coverage and began to beseech God.

The first prayer request is for salvation and spiritual growth. I ask God to open Dean's eyes and heart to his need for a Savior, and I pray for him to love God with all his heart, soul, mind, and strength: *Lord, give him a love for Your Word, a desire to read and obey it, and a passion for prayer.* I ask for Dean to be a man after God's own heart, have the mind of Christ, and surrender his will to the Holy Spirit's leading. I petition God to give my husband a hatred for sin and a growing discernment of right and wrong.

You get the idea; I pray Scripture for my husband, believing God's Word won't return void and also believing God answers every prayer according to His will. "This is the confidence we have in approaching God: that if we ask anything according to his will, he hears us. And if we know that he hears us—whatever we ask— we know that we have what we asked of him" (1 John 5:14-15). I'm confident that when I pray from the Bible, I'm praying God's will. I have His promise of an answer.

I've prayed for my husband for about 20 years and have seen many answers.

I encourage you to collect your own scriptures that are appropriate to your situation. Keep them in a notebook, card file, or prayer journal. I used a concordance at first, but I continue to add scriptures to my prayers that speak to me regarding the circumstances. I also like to pray Paul's prayers found in Eph. 1:15-23; 3:14-21; Phil. 1:9-11; and Col. 1:9-12.

I've prayed for my husband for about 20 years and have seen many answers. When faced with important issues, I talk to God, and He often aligns my heart and Dean's. I don't pray anything for Dean that I wouldn't pray for myself. As I pray for him, God changes me. I love this man profoundly and treasure who he is and who he's becoming.

My friend Susie desperately wanted her husband, Alex, to be a godly man; therefore, as most good wives do, she nagged, prodded, and hinted at how he could accomplish the goal. Life was transformed when she quit preaching and started praying. We accomplish more on our knees than anywhere else. As you can imagine, both she and Alex are happier now.

Prayer request number two is for our marriage. Since marriage represents Christ's relationship to the Church (Eph. 5:32), and since God wants Christian marriages to paint that picture to the world, I pray for Dean to love me as Christ loves the Church (v. 25). I pray I'll submit to him, honor him, and be a true helpmate. I ask God to protect our relationship. Again, hit the concordance and find verses relating to marriage. Remember—if it's His will, He'll answer.

However, I've discovered God's timetable is rarely the same as mine. So I can't give up, though I've wanted to more than once. I heard a pastor say, "Mathematically speaking, if 1,000 years is as a day to God, then 10 years to us equals approximately 15 minutes on God's watch." When these last two decades seem like an eternity, I remind myself that it's been but a short 30 minutes to God. Half an hour isn't long and gives me a better perspective on asking, seeking, and knocking. Another reminder I repeat often is "God loves my spouse as much as I do and longs for his salvation with as much fervor. It's His heart's desire."

Marriage is a covenant relationship, and I believe it's near and dear to God's heart. As I said earlier, each Christian marriage is a depiction of Christ's relationship to His Bride, the Church. I know God yearns for our marriages to mirror His love for us.

Monica longed to be cherished by her husband, Steve. As my friend lifted this request to God for a tender, romantic husband, she noticed Steve becoming more thoughtful and caring in the little things. Her heart rejoiced not only in being cherished but also in God's goodness. I believe God wants to answer these kinds of prayers, because the result brings Him glory.

Third, I beseech God to teach Dean and me to parent according to His plan. Paul admonished the Ephesian fathers not to exasperate their children and warned the Colossians not to embitter theirs. God's instructions that we parents teach, train, mature, and control our kids have become matters of prayer in my life. I also pray for the relationships we have with our children to be filled with love, respect, and encouragement.

Even though Marcy's husband, John, doesn't attend church, God has given him a real concern for his children's spiritual well-being—in accordance with his wife's prayer. "John not only encourages them in their church attendance but also is willing to pay for Christian school, mission trips, and camps," Marcy gratefully said. She gives God all the credit.

Prayer for extended family is the fourth area I cover. Many in our extended family do not have personal relationships with Jesus Christ. I pray for the members of my immediate family to be lights in their dark world, but more important, I pray for us to love them with God's love, be available to them in their times of need, and enjoy a rich relationship with each of them.

God has provided those answers. Dean and I have good relationships with all 10 of his siblings, their spouses, and his 23 nieces and nephews. Many are married now, and there are 34 great-nieces and -nephews. I can't tell you how much we love each member of his family, and I know it's a "God thing." I pray for them each by name every week, that none will perish and God will draw each of them to himself, and I'm just now seeing the fruit of 20-plus years of prayer.

My fifth request is for Dean's friends and friendships. I not only ask God to protect Dean from bad company who corrupt good morals (1 Cor. 15:33) but also ask Him to surround my spouse with godly men whose hearts are fully His. I desire, just as God does, for my husband to be a friend who loves at all times (Prov. 17:17) and to have men in his life who will do the same.

As you may have noticed, the first five requests all involve relationships. The next five focus on what's going on in Dean's life.

The sixth prayer request is for Dean's job. I pray for safety and protection while he's at work. Also, I thank God for His provision and ask Him to continue to meet all our needs according to His glorious riches in Christ Jesus (Phil. 4:19).

Prayer request number seven is for stewardship. I pray for Dean to make wise use of his time, money, and possessions. I also ask that he give not reluctantly but cheerfully, and in all honesty, my husband is the most generous person I've ever known. He's not only willing to tithe but also would give anybody the shirt off his back.

Marcy ached to give 10 percent of the family income, but John hadn't reached that point. Her pastor assured her that God looks on the heart. "If a woman can't tithe because of an unbelieving or unwilling spouse, God takes into account the desire and blesses her accordingly." Marcy felt better but continued to pray. After a year or so, she asked John again, and that time he said yes.

Dean is my priority above church and second only to God. When I honor my husband, I honor God.

Prayer for Dean's health is the eighth area I cover. I lift up any ailments he might be experiencing, and then I just ask God to give him a long and healthy life. I want to grow old with this man, so I ask God to grant us many years of health to serve Him.

Number nine is for Dean's mind. "Do not conform any longer to the pattern of this world, but be transformed by the renewing of your mind" (Rom. 12:2). I ask God to renew my husband's mind daily, to teach him to take captive his thoughts, and to teach him to choose to think about things that are true, right, and pure (Phil. 4:8.) I pray that Dean will forgive when he's hurt so bitterness won't take root in his life.

I ask God to renew my husband's mind daily, to teach him to take captive his thoughts, and to teach him to choose to think about things that are true, right, and pure.

Ellen and David received more than $10,000 in one lump sum after living from paycheck to paycheck for more than a decade. "I wanted to pay off our credit card debt and be free from the high interest rate," shared Ellen, "but David just wanted to have money in the bank—a new sensation for us. After trying to reason with him about the logic of paying 14 percent while earning much less, I decided to shut up and pray. Within a week, David said he realized we would benefit more if we paid off our debt. I knew God had heard my frustrated prayers."

Last, I pray for my husband to be a man of integrity. I pray he'll make the right choice, the honest choice, whether or not anyone is looking. Just how faithfully God has answered this prayer was brought to my attention recently. Our son Adam is applying to law school, and in his personal statement he mentioned how honesty and integrity had been modeled for him repeatedly in the daily choices his dad lived out. *Thank You, Lord, for the example Dean has provided to our three kids.*

IN SUMMARY

Now lest you think I'm some sort of perfect prayer

warrior who has it all figured out and never tires, let me assure you that's far from reality. I've become discouraged over the years, thrown in the prayer shawl a few times, and resigned more than once. God's clock is set in a different time zone, and though patience may be a virtue, it's not one of mine.

The first time I decided that nothing in my life ever changed and prayer was not only a waste of breath but also a huge waste of time, God led me to 1 Sam. 12:23: "As for me, far be it from me that I should sin against the Lord by failing to pray for you." I saw that prayer isn't an option in my life, because not praying equals sin. The result is God's business, but the act of prayer is my responsibility. That truth hit right smack in the middle of my heart. E. M. Bounds said, "Our praying, however, needs to be pressed and pursued with an energy that never tires, a persistency which will not be denied, and a courage which never fails."*

Remember Aaron and Ur in the Old Testament? They assisted Moses, actually holding up his arms when he was too tired to continue. You see, the Israelites were in a heated battle, and when Moses kept his hands raised toward heaven, they dominated. But when he dropped his arms of sheer exhaustion, God's chosen people moved to the losing side of the war. As I mentioned in the friendship chapter and will reiterate here, we all need an Aaron and an Ur in our lives, because there will come a time when we can't walk a step farther without aid from someone.

Another time when I felt discouraged and wanted to give up but knew I couldn't, God led me to an obscure verse that has become one of my favorites regarding prayer: "Epaphras, who is one of you and a servant of Christ Jesus,

---

*Internet Source

sends greetings. He is always wrestling in prayer for you, that you may stand firm in all the will of God, mature and fully assured" (Col. 4:12). Epaphras wrestled in prayer so his people would stand firm and be mature. I need to stand in the gap for my husband, because if Epaphras's prayers made a difference, so do mine. His example also encourages me to pray big, just as he did.

Evangelist Luis Palau said, "You can read all the manuals on prayer and listen to other people pray, but until you begin to pray yourself, you will never understand prayer. It's like riding a bicycle or swimming: You learn by doing."*

So don't be afraid, because practice makes prayer warriors, and prayer warriors invest in lives. Prayer changes hearts, makes the impossible possible, and gives hope to the hopeless. Prayer moves us to God dependency, and that's exactly where He wants us.

PICTURES FROM GOD'S WORD

Elijah showed more guts and gumption than many of us ever will. When the rubber of his faith met the pavement of life, this man didn't disappoint God. Let's look at his story.

Elijah the Tishbite followed God's instructions and met with Ahab, Israel's king. Elijah confronted the king by saying to him, "You have abandoned the LORD's commands and have followed the Baals" (1 Kings 18:18). He directed King Ahab to gather people from all over Israel and meet him on Mount Carmel. "And bring the four hundred and fifty prophets of Baal and the four hundred prophets of Asherah" (v. 19).

While Ahab assembled his entourage, "Elijah went before the people and said, 'How long will you waver between

---

*Internet Source

two opinions? If the LORD is God, follow him; but if Baal is God, follow him.' But the people said nothing" (v. 21). Elijah pointed out the fact that there was only one of him but 450 prophets of Baal. Then he laid a challenge before them.

"Get two bulls for us. Let them choose one for themselves, and let them cut it into pieces and put it on the wood but not set fire to it. I will prepare the other bull and put it on the wood but not set fire to it. Then you call on the name of your god, and I will call on the name of the LORD. The god who answers by fire—he is God" (vv. 23-24). The people agreed.

Elijah invited the Baals to be first, so they chose and prepared their bull. They called on the name of Baal from morning until noon; they shouted, they danced around the altar, but he never answered. "At noon Elijah began to taunt them. 'Shout louder!' he said. 'Surely he is a god! Perhaps he is deep in thought, or busy, or traveling. Maybe he is sleeping and must be awakened'" (v. 27). They shouted even louder, and following their custom, they slashed themselves with swords and spears. They continued frantically until evening.

Then Elijah called the people over to him. Taking 12 stones, one for each of Israel's tribes, he built an altar in the Lord's name. Around the altar he dug a trench big enough to hold about 13 gallons of water. Then he arranged the wood, sliced the bull, and placed it on the timber. After everything appeared ready, he requested four large jars of water. Three times he had water poured over the sacrifice and the wood. Water dripped from the altar and filled the trench.

Now Elijah was ready to show what his God could do. He stepped forward and prayed. "O LORD, God of Abraham, Isaac and Israel, let it be known today that you are God in Israel and that I am your servant and have done all these things at your command. Answer me, O LORD, answer me, so these people will know that you, O LORD, are God, and that you are turning their hearts back again" (vv. 36-37).

The fire of the Lord came down from heaven, consuming everything—the bull, the wood, the stones, the water, and even the surrounding soil. The Israelites fell prostrate, declaring God to be the one true God.

What faith Elijah had! In our next examination of Scripture, the disciples seemed like a pretty faithless and often clueless bunch, at least until after Jesus ascended to heaven following the Resurrection.

Matthew 17 tells the story of a father with an epileptic son who had sought out the help of the disciples, but they had been unable to assist. The son often fell into fire or water and suffered greatly. When the disciples failed to heal the child, the father turned to Jesus.

"'O unbelieving and perverse generation,' Jesus replied, 'how long shall I stay with you? How long shall I put up with you? Bring the boy here to me.' Jesus rebuked the demon, and it came out of the boy, and he was healed from that moment" (vv. 17-18).

Later the disciples asked Jesus privately why they had been unable to heal the boy. "Because you have so little faith. I tell you the truth, if you have faith as small as a mustard seed, you can say to this mountain, 'Move from here to there' and it will move. Nothing will be impossible for you" (v. 20).

Faith is a key ingredient to our prayer life. Heb. 11:6 says, "Without faith it is impossible to please God." We must believe—not necessarily that He will, but that He can. Ultimately He chooses whether or not He answers our prayers, responding with a yes, a no, or a wait, but we must know deep in our hearts that He is more than able.

PONDERING GOD'S WORD

- "Unless the LORD builds the [family], its builders labor in vain. Unless the LORD watches over the [family], the watchmen stand guard in vain" (Ps. 127:1).
- "Lord, teach us to pray, just as John taught his disciples" (Luke 11:1).
- "Elijah was a man just like us. He prayed earnestly that it would not rain, and it did not rain on the land for three and a half years. Again he prayed, and the heavens gave rain, and the earth produced its crops" (James 5:17-18).
- "Ask and it will be given to you; seek and you will find; knock and the door will be opened to you" (Matt. 7:7).
- "You may ask me for anything in my name, and I will do it" (John 14:14).

Father God,

As I pray for my husband, family, and friends, may I come boldly before Your throne of grace, knowing that You can do all I ask and so much more. I don't need to fear the outcome, because You promise that You always have my very best in mind. I ask You to give me the faith of Elijah and the courage to boldly show You off as he did.

Would You direct me as I pray for Dean? Please continue to teach me more and more about prayer. I count kneeling before You a great privilege and honor. How blessed I am that the Lord of Lords and King of Kings is willing to listen to my pleas and that You so graciously answer my requests. You bid me to come into Your presence, sit at Your feet, and share my hopes, my fears, my needs.

May I never take for granted the freedom to pray anytime at any place. I thank You that the more I pray, the more I'm changed. The more I pray, the more compassion and kindness I bestow. The more I pray, the more I look like Jesus. Please give me a love for Your Word, a love for prayer, and Your love for people.

It's in Christ's name I ask. Amen.

Listening to God's Voice

What would God have you pray for your husband?

_____

_____

_____

_____

_____

_____

_____

_____

_____

_____

_____

_____

_____

8

Monkey See, Monkey Do
The Kids Are Watching

"Mom, Dad, I'm pregnant." Tori closed her eyes, hoping to shut out the hurt and disappointment etched on her parents' faces. She knew she had let them down.

Her mom's sobs started just a split second ahead of her dad's yelling.

"How could you? How could you disgrace us like that? I knew Johnny was a no-good bum. Wait until I get my hands on him! He'll be marching down the aisle in a tux so fast it'll make your head swim. What were you thinking? I thought your mother took you to church so you wouldn't do something like this!"

Because Tori and her mom and sister had attended church and Sunday School regularly when she was a child, her dad expected it to still impact her life.

"I haven't been to church since I was 10 years old, and all I remember are stories about arks, rainbows, and Moses. I don't even know if they're true!"

"How can you say that?" Tori's mother said, sobbing harder. "Just because you don't go to church doesn't mean you stop believing."

Debbie now realizes that by dropping out of church, her daughters failed to gain a firm foundation in the Lord. After growing weary of going alone, she gave in to the disappointment and quit going altogether.

"I always thought I would start back in a few months," Debbie said. "I just needed a break. It's hard to go alone. The months turned into years. I just assumed the kids would be OK. Because my faith was solid, I fooled myself into believing theirs was too. Tori's unwanted pregnancy woke me up to the truth.

"But not right away. At first I felt too angry to see the whole picture. When Tori lost the baby in her fourth month, I knew we all needed healing. I dragged the girls back to church. I didn't want Roni to repeat her sister's mistake.

"God opened my eyes over the next couple of years." Debbie sighed. "The first mistake I made was to grow weary in doing good. Quitting was easier, and I assumed I could raise Christian kids who embraced Christian principles without going to church. I've since discovered that it's tough to raise godly kids even if they go to church every single week."

Debbie regrets her decision to leave the girls so vulnerable to the world's influence. Though she has no guarantee anything would have been different, she believes keeping them in church would have at least given Tori a fighting chance. Since God's Word changes hearts and lives, Tori would have been impacted by truth on a weekly basis.

I'm amazed to discover how many families drop out of church during the most crucial years in their children's existence. Church isn't the end-all answer to everything, but I agree with Debbie's observation that raising moral kids in an immoral world takes all the help we can get.

Being a visionary is difficult, especially if no one else shares the vision. The deepest desire of my heart was to raise godly kids who love the Lord. No small feat for anyone, the task doubles in size when attempted alone. As an unequally yoked parent, I'm the lone spiritual role model. Faithfulness in my walk is imperative. My children create accountability in my life. My calling is to live a life that's honoring to God on a daily basis. They're watching and listening, and my actions speak to them in ways mere words cannot. Knowing this has kept me on the straight-and-narrow path even when I wanted to veer.

Every choice I make and every word I say has the power to affect my kids' perception of God and the life they'll ultimately live.

I owe it to my kids to be real. I've seen a few hypocrites in my day, and I prayed to be the same woman Monday through Saturday that I am on Sunday morning. Through prayer, God enables me to see the big picture. Not just what this will mean to me now, but how it will affect my kids in the future. I have made my share of mistakes, but constant prayer for guidance and wisdom has saved me from getting off track many times.

We had some friends who lied to save money on a business deal. Now, years later, their adult children don't think twice about lying to achieve the desired result. What our friends did once, their children adopted as a lifestyle. God impressed that lesson on my heart. Every choice I make and every word I say has the power to affect my kids' perception of God and the life they'll ultimately live. *O dear Father, give me the strength to remain faithful.*

Rachel is bulimic. Her mom, Cindy, is a lovely Christian woman who is fanatical about her health and does various exercises for half an hour every single morning. Sadly, the message Rachel receives from her mother is that there's nothing more important than size, shape, and fat intake. Cindy admits to being more devoted to her health regime than her spiritual growth. She's heart-broken and feels responsible for Rachel's current struggles with food and self-image. "How I wish she had seen me on my knees every morning instead of on the treadmill!"

GROWING UP IN CHURCH DOESN'T NECESSARILY MAKE GODLY TEENAGERS

I've spent much of the past decade working with high school and college girls, and it's a big mistake for Christian parents to think that just because their kids are growing up in church, they'll be fine. In all honesty, I once assumed the same thing. The truth is that these teens face the same temptations as the rest of the world: drinking, sex, lying, swearing, drugs, and all the rest. God trusted Adam and Eve, but they still went for the fruit.

A young lady I know started attending school parties when she was a freshman. Determined not to drink or get into trouble, Mandy just wanted to have fun and fit in. One Friday night at a post-football-game party, a group of lesbians slipped a drug into her soda and molested her. Her parents' trust didn't save her from this tragedy. It's not about trust—this just isn't the world we grew up in.

The Christian life is about a relationship with Jesus Christ. It's not about church attendance—though that's extremely important. It's not about rules. We need to pray with our kids and for our kids. As we're instructed in Deuteronomy, we need to share God with them while they're sitting, standing, lying down, and walking by the wayside. I don't mean nagging or preaching. I'm talking about transparency, vulnerability, and honesty.

I feel so passionate about this because it's an area in which I failed. We did share some and pray some, but I presented God more as a set of rules than the God who loves them so completely. In John's Gospel we read these words of Jesus: "If you love me, you will obey what I command" (14:15). I used to think obedience meant I loved Him. I now realize it's because I love Him that I yearn to obey. Our kids need to have a love relationship with Jesus. Teacher Beth Moore says this is the number one prayer she prays for her daughters. If they fervently love Him, the rest of their lives will fall more easily into place.

I once heard a pastor say, "If Satan can't keep you from salvation, his next goal is to keep you from victory." Maybe he can't ruin our eternity, but he'll sure try to destroy our testimony. Often when our kids fall, their testimony to their unbelieving fathers, friends, and relatives is damaged. I believe that kids growing up in the church are more vulnerable, because there's an enemy looking for someone to devour.

Building Faith from Daily Life

Matt had just returned from a trip through California with his choir, and we were driving home from church where I had met his bus. "Mom," Matt said as we drove along, "I think God wants me to go to a Christian college." He named a specific school they had visited on their trip.

I was floored. I had dared my kids to dream big. After all, if I could be a writer, nothing lay beyond their reach— nothing, that is, if God is in it. But my becoming a rocket scientist seemed more feasible to my small thinking, given our finances.

So I calmly said, "We'll pray about the possibility and see what God does." Truthfully I didn't see how God could pull this one off. We had no extra money over and above our living expenses, no rich relatives hanging on our family tree, and Christian college, especially in California, is quite expensive.

Matt and I prayed for the next year, both of us growing more certain that this was God's plan for him. At the beginning of his senior year, we discussed it with his dad, and God bless Dean's generous heart—even though he didn't know how we would do it, he was willing to give it a try. We sent our son off to college on a wing and a prayer.

God will not ask you to do something and not pave the way.

I'm here to tell you, God will not ask you to do something and not pave the way. He not only changed my heart and Dean's but also provided the funding. Every single month we scraped together another college tuition payment! I'm again reminded that nothing is impossible with God.

One way we can make Christ real to our kids is daring them to dream. I've come to believe that we parents are often the weight that keeps our kids' faith from soaring. Sometimes I find myself fearing God will let me down when I challenge my kids to go boldly to Him.

I remember another time in Matt's life when praying stretched me more than him.

"Mom, my book bag is gone!" Near tears, fear showing in his eyes, he greeted me where I waited for him in the car.

I jumped out, and we rushed back to the baseball field where his team had just finished practice. "Where did you leave it?" I asked, my gaze searching the grassy surroundings.

"I left it right here at the edge of the field with everyone else's." His brown eyes filled with angst. "I had 10 of those coupon books I'm supposed to sell for student senate."

"Oh, Matt!" Now I wanted to cry.

"I'll have to pay for them." Not much of a saver, this

expense would leave Matt's account at the credit union in the red.

"Let's pray." I attempted to sound enthusiastic and hopeful but felt neither. "We'll ask God to return your bag with everything still in it." *Now, Jeri, that's about as likely as pigs learning ballet. What junior higher dishonest enough to steal would return valuable coupon books that he could sell and then pocket the money?*

I yearned for faith, but honestly, I didn't think even God could handle this one. Matt and I prayed on the drive home, and then he called his youth pastor and asked him to pray. I called good old reliable Kathy and Val. If nothing else, we had a whole lot of praying going on.

The next morning Matt's bag was returned with everything still in it! Even with my weak and pathetic faith, God did a miracle.

For our kids to grow, we have to grow. Remember that old saying about a student being able to go only as far as the teacher? If I desire Christlikeness for my children, I must seek it for myself. I'm the only example they have. I want to echo Paul: "Follow my example, as I follow the example of Christ" (1 Cor. 11:1). Monkey see, monkey do. May my monkeys find a faithful example in me.

A Look at Scripture

In Acts, Luke tells us that Timothy's mother "was a Jewess and a believer, but [his] father was a Greek" (16:1). From this information most Bible scholars agree Timothy grew up in an unequally yoked home. Paul presents us with more information in his second letter to Timothy: "I have been reminded of your sincere faith, which first lived in your grandmother Lois and in your mother Eunice and, I am persuaded, now lives in you also" (1:5).

Timothy's grandmother and mother passed their faith down to him. This gives me hope! I can just picture these two women pouring themselves into this little boy, praying with him and sharing Bible stories as they tucked him into bed at night.

Sometimes the task overwhelms me, but these two women succeeded in raising a godly man. I think God revealed this information to give women like you and me a hope to grasp onto. He doesn't tell us much, but He tells us enough to assure us that it's possible to raise godly offspring, even if there's only one of us carrying out the daunting task.

God provides another example of a man, a judge and high priest, whose sons were less than honorable. Eli, a servant of the most high God, failed to raise children who loved and honored God. "Eli's sons were wicked men; they had no regard for the LORD" (1 Sam. 2:12).

That wasn't the biggest problem, however. The larger issue was that Eli knew and ignored their behavior. Unhappy with the situation, God asked, "Why do you honor your sons more than me?" (v. 29). Later, the Lord spoke to Samuel saying, "I told him [Eli] that I would judge his family forever because of the sin he knew about; his sons made themselves contemptible, and he failed to restrain them" (3:13). God removed His blessing from Eli's family.

In the early 1980s I went through a Bible study on godly women. Recently I thumbed through the chapter on mothering. The question "In what ways have your children been a spiritual blessing to you?" caught my eye. After all these years, my answer remains the same: "It is for them that I keep going when otherwise I would have given up." Thank you, Matt, Kelsy, and Adam, for keeping me in the race. No matter how old our children are, they need to find us faithful.

Pondering God's Word

- "Whatever you have learned or received or heard from me, or seen in me—put it into practice. And the God of peace will be with you" (Phil. 4:9).
- "I prayed for this child, and the LORD has granted me what I asked of him. So now I give him to the LORD. For his whole life he will be given over to the LORD" (1 Sam. 1:27-28).
- "Train a child in the way he should go, and when he is old he will not turn from it" (Prov. 22:6).
- "Sons are a heritage from the LORD, children a reward from him" (Ps. 127:3).
- "Discipline your son, and he will give you peace; he will bring delight to your soul" (Prov. 29:17).

Abba Father,

Reveal to my heart the secret of raising godly offspring. I yearn to be a Eunice and a Lois, not an Eli. Teach me to pass my faith on to others. Keep me diligent in the things that matter: quiet times, church attendance, my testimony. When I grow weary, enable me to keep on so I might reap a harvest of blessing.

I also pray that my life will be genuine, that I'll be the same person no matter who's watching or who isn't. May my children see authentic Christianity in me and an abiding love for You. I pray that You'll be my number one priority and that the picture my actions paint will confirm that as truth. I need Your wisdom, Your strength, and Your guidance. I'm not foolish enough to think I stand a chance without Your leading the way.

May my kids love You with all their hearts, souls, minds, and strength. Give them each a heart after Your heart, the mind of Christ, and a will submitted to the authority of the Holy Spirit. It's in the strong name of Jesus I pray. Amen.

Listening to God's Voice

Ask God what He wants you to pray for your children. Write each child's name below followed by those prayer needs.

_____

_____

_____

_____

_____

_____

_____

_____

_____

_____

_____

_____

_____

_____

9

My Empty Pew
Combating Loneliness

Climbing into the car, I pasted on a brave smile and waved. "Bye, Sweetie," I called out the window, swallowing hard to dissolve the lump in my throat. As I pulled out of the driveway, I watched my husband through the rearview mirror, growing smaller and farther away. That picture depicted exactly how I felt on Sundays; our marriage grew small and far away with miles between us. I longed to share the most important part of my life, Jesus, with the most important person in my life, my husband.

Once again, I was driving to church alone. Going to church by myself was the hardest thing I did all week, much more difficult at this point than when the kids were small and lived at home. They gave me accountability, a reason to go, and someone to sit with. Now I looked for excuses to stay home.

I always arrived after the service began. That way I didn't have to greet everyone with a happy smile and tell people, "I'm fine," when in truth I didn't feel fine at all. My heart grieved. This unequally yoked life is a lonesome trek. After 22 years of walking alone in my Christianity, a large chunk of my life is separate from my spouse's—lived singly. Sadly, Dean barely knows most of my Christian friends.

Spiritual singleness is a difficult role. Churches everywhere include married people who walk alone in their relationship with God. Their spouses either lack commitment or do not believe. I was not as alone in this as I sometimes felt, and though it's a solitary trek, I've learned that certain choices make it easier.

KNOWING MY LIMITATIONS

I avoid Sunday School classes for married adults, which only depress me and make contentment more difficult to achieve. For me, it's like a magnifying glass, enlarging my grief and my total, complete aloneness. I also shun sad movies, because they leave me feeling down for days. I figure life's sad enough—why torture myself? In other words, I know myself, and I don't invite unnecessary struggles.

Kathy always enjoyed her class for married adults, even though her husband stayed home. I used to tease her, accusing her of being a Pollyanna. Attending a couples' event alone didn't daunt her. For me, it was worse than having surgery without anesthesia. So I play it safe and veer toward women's ministry events. All the women are there alone, so it's not an issue.

Since my kids are grown and gone from home, I also avoid family affairs. They only serve to remind me that my nest is empty and I walk alone with God. I attend a small church and am the only person without either a husband or a child. My pew is completely empty, except for me, and since adapting to a vacant nest has been a difficult adjustment in my life, I avoid tormenting myself more.

For me to feel I fit in, I needed to be involved in the service. I started by teaching a preschool Sunday School class. Since then, I've taught women, high school girls, and college girls. This is my niche, and I encourage you to find yours. Helping gives me a reason to get to church on Sundays, a place to belong, and a sense of purpose bigger than myself.

Every church has unfilled positions and needs more assistance. Ask God where He's sending you. It's commonly said that in any church 20 percent of the parishioners do 80 percent of the work. Think of the possibilities—nursery work, choir, hospital visitation. The list is limitless. Maybe God will use your gifts to start something new.

Agony and Ecstasy

"I think I'll go with you today," Ted informed Krista as she started out the door one Sunday morning.

Her stomach knotted. She glanced at him, wondering what brought this on. "Sure."

"I'll change my shirt and be right out."

Joy and dread warred within her. Every time Ted attended church her hopes soared. *Is this the day he'll ask Jesus into his life? Will this be the first of many weeks we'll sit in church together? Will anyone talk to him? Will he hate the sermon? The music?* At best, the experience was bittersweet.

On the drive, Krista rubbed sweaty palms against her cotton skirt, praying fervently in silence. *God, please help him feel comfortable, and send men to shake his hand. Let the pastor's message pierce his heart with truth. Open his eyes to see his need for You.* Her endless, noiseless begging continued as she walked toward the double doors.

"Where would you like to sit?" she whispered. No use dragging him up to the front, where she normally settled into one of the first five rows. He would definitely be intimidated then.

Ted pointed to the last row. Krista nodded and slipped into the second chair, leaving him the seat on the end. Her hands, balled tightly into fists, rested in her lap. Her tension mounted as the praise team took the stage.

"I was a wreck, scrutinizing everything," Krista commented afterward. "Every word the pastor uttered—I wondered how Ted interpreted it. I left with a headache, a stomachache, and wondered if my life would be easier if he just stayed home. His coming along put me on an emotional roller coaster that left me exhausted and depressed.

"I wished the pastor had said this instead of that, wished the man sitting in front of us was friendlier, and wished the associate minister who prayed for the offering had foregone his minisermon about tithing. I already knew how Ted felt about church and money issues.

My spouse's church attendance and salvation are God's work, not mine.

"Anyway," Krista continued, catching her breath, "one day the truth hit me. I wasn't trusting God! Startled by the revelation, I cried. I needed to relax and not worry about all the details. God is sovereign, and He's big enough to handle the particulars. This concept brought freedom. I still pray for God to take charge of everything said and done, but then I just enjoy the service. God can and will do the rest."

I resided at the opposite end of the spectrum from Krista. In the early years I invited Dean to church often. If he went, I usually ended up regretting I had asked, because he was miserable. When he said no, disappointment and sorrow nearly did me in. Either way, I lost, so I quit mentioning it.

I adopted a new policy: I would invite him only for special events and programs the kids were involved in unless the Holy Spirit directed otherwise. I would ask without pressure or expectation and pray for sensitivity to accept Dean's answer graciously and trust the Lord for His timing. My spouse's church attendance and salvation are God's work, not mine.

WHEN GOD DOESN'T MAKE SENSE

Adam is our youngest son, and it was during his senior

year of high school that I felt God tugging at my heart. He wanted me to change churches! Now I'm a woman who likes stability. Dean and I have lived in the same house since before Adam's birth. We drive a car we've owned since Adam was five. You're getting the picture—change doesn't come easy or often. And now God wanted my co-operation in willingly seeking a new Body of Believers to fellowship with.

This season held grief, tears, and confusion. I left behind the only church home I had known as an adult, the place my kids grew up, the place all three of them started their journeys with Christ. I had been employed there, and the staff and I were on a first-name basis. But hardest of all, I had to resign a teaching ministry in the women's program that I loved, ministry that bore fruit.

I didn't understand why God would strip me of everything comfortable and familiar during the difficult time of sending our youngest out of state for college. As I visited other churches, seeking where God wanted me, I sensed God's will was a small church crammed full of large families. Kids filled every nook and cranny. *Why here, God?* My aloneness intensified.

I obeyed and joined that little Body of Believers, kicking and screaming all the way. Hindsight is wonderful. Looking back, I understand at least two reasons why God moved me, but I can honestly say it didn't make sense at the time. His will makes perfect sense now.

The first reason was for Dean. My new pastor, Sam, was a cowboy who wore a pair of boots every Sunday. Those boots helped my husband feel comfortable. Sam prayed for Dean and reached out to him on numerous occasions. At my old church only two men in nearly 17 years ever extended a hand of friendship and welcome.

The second reason was for me. God knew I would

need the accountability a small church affords. As I mentioned earlier, going completely alone turned into a huge struggle for me. I needed people who noticed when I didn't show up, people who would call on Monday morning and say, "Hey, where were you? I missed you." So God's crazy idea wasn't so crazy after all; He knows me better than I know myself.

Find your place in a church where you're comfortable, trust your hubby's church participation to God, and don't sweat the details.

As women alone on a spiritual journey, we need to prayerfully figure out what works for each of us. Find your place in a church where you're comfortable, trust your hubby's church participation to God, and don't sweat the details. Last, trust God even if the way He's leading makes little sense at the time. He truly knows best.

TWO SCRIPTURAL EXAMPLES

Now we'll look at Scripture to examine the ways two Bible characters dealt with loneliness. The first fellow, John, referred to himself as "the disciple whom Jesus loved" (John 13:23; 21:7, 20). The son of Zebedee, the brother of James, and a fisherman by trade, this man, along with Peter and his brother James, became Christ's closest friend and confidant. He was the one whom Jesus entrusted with His mother's care upon His death.

So John knew the richness of sweet fellowship both during Christ's life as one of the 12 disciples and after Christ's death as one of the apostles who continued tirelessly to spread the gospel. In Acts we see him joining Peter on a mission trip to Samaria and praying with other believers. In Galatians he's referred to as a pillar.

Yet at the end of John's life we find him in exile and very much alone. "I, John, your brother and companion in the suffering and kingdom and patient endurance that are ours in Jesus, was on the island of Patmos because of the word of God and the testimony of Jesus" (Rev. 1:9). Apparently sent there for sharing his faith, John wrote the Book of Revelation from that isolated island.

I'm so impressed because, unlike me, John made the best of a bad situation. He wasn't questioning, complaining, or throwing a pity party for himself. He used his loneliness wisely, at the feet of God, receiving divine revelation, recording what he saw, and sending the scrolls to the seven churches in Ephesus, Smyrna, Pergamum, Thyatira, Sardis, Philadelphia, and Laodicea.

Solomon, on the other hand, tried to fill the lonely, empty places in his life with everything but God. He was David and Bathsheba's second child. Though David's life of spiritual faithfulness for the most part gave Solomon a solid example, the boy also grew up in a home where polygamy was practiced and jealousy and strife were evident.

Solomon started his reign well, but his first foolish mistake was choosing a pagan king's daughter for his wife. This choice began his moral decline. Then God appeared to him in a vision and encouraged him to ask for whatever he wished. Admitting his weakness and ignorance, he requested a discerning heart. Pleased with Solomon's wise selection, God not only granted his petition but also promised him that he would be the wisest of men and obtain great riches and honor as well.

As his wealth and fame increased, Solomon loved the splendor. He developed a taste for luxury and led an extravagant lifestyle. Marrying foreign women, he became excessively sensual. His many wives influenced him to sanctify idolatry, and eventually he even oppressed the people of Israel.

Though he was known as the wisest man, his decision to fill his emptiness with more—more women, more sex, more material possessions—proved to be a bad choice. According to one Bible scholar, "Solomon's description of a fool in Proverbs is a vivid picture of his own failings."*
I believe each of us has a void in our lives that only God can fill. Instead of letting God fill his void, Solomon found himself empty, and the more he acquired, the emptier he became.

Most believe Solomon is the author of Ecclesiastes. Let's look at the words he penned there: "'Meaningless! Meaningless!' says the Teacher. 'Utterly meaningless! Everything is meaningless'" (1:2). "Whoever loves money never has money enough; whoever loves wealth is never satisfied with his income" (5:10). This man had everything yet found satisfaction in nothing.

He ends his philosophical musing with this key verse: "Now all has been heard; here is the conclusion of the matter: Fear God and keep his commandments, for this is the whole duty of man" (12:13). I wonder how differently his life might have turned out had he taken his own good advice.

Whether your life is filled to overflowing with people or you are in a season of isolation, choose to fill your voids with God alone. I've made both choices, having searched for answers in the things of this world and letting God be my all in all. Only in Him did I find peace, contentment, and joy—even in my empty pew.

Thompson Chain Reference Bible, New International Version. Copyright 1983 by the B. B. Kirkbride Bible Company, Inc., Indianapolis, Ind., and the Zondervan Corporation, Grand Rapids. "Character Studies," 1558.

PONDERING GOD'S WORD

- "Let us consider how we may spur one another on toward love and good deeds. Let us not give up meeting together, as some are in the habit of doing, but let us encourage one another—and all the more as you see the Day approaching" (Heb. 10:24-25).
- "'I know the plans I have for you,' declares the LORD, 'plans to prosper you and not to harm you, plans to give you hope and a future'" (Jer. 29:11).
- "God has said, 'Never will I leave you; never will I forsake you'" (Heb. 13:5).
- "A time is coming, and has come, when you will be scattered, each to his own home. You will leave me all alone. Yet I am not alone, for my Father is with me" (John 16:32).
- "O LORD, do not forsake me; be not far from me, O my God" (Ps. 38:21).

Dearest Father,

Please be with me in those lonely times that naturally arise out of an unequally yoked relationship. Make me aware of my limitations, and give me the wisdom to choose wisely the activities that will enhance my growth and not cause me to stumble. And God, please reveal where You want me to serve in Your Body of Believers.

On the occasions my husband does attend church, I invite You to be in charge instead of me. Teach me to rest, knowing You are there with me. Open my spouse's ears to hear what You know he's ready to hear. Lay upon the hearts of men to reach out to him, and, Father, flood me with Your peace, that I may rest in You.

I long to follow where You lead, so don't let fear or lack of understanding paralyze me. May my trust be in You alone, knowing that You're completely trustworthy. The plans You have for me are for my best, even when it doesn't seem that way at the time. I thank You, my dearest and most faithful companion, for Your promise to never leave me. I love You, Lord. In Your name I pray. Amen.

Listening to God's Voice

Father, what are you saying to me regarding my lonely times?

_____

_____

_____

_____

_____

_____

_____

_____

_____

_____

_____

_____

_____

_____

10
Pride and Prejudice
Battling Self-Righteous Attitudes

About three years ago I participated in my first Beth Moore Bible study, *A Woman's Heart: God's Dwelling Place*. This book sent me digging through the Word, and God sent me digging through my heart. It's not always pleasant and is often painful, but the result is always life-changing.

About halfway through the study, God removed a veil from my eyes, and I saw something I had never seen before. I had a prideful, arrogant attitude toward Dean. The truth, as clear as a freshly cleaned windowpane, broke my heart. Even now, after three years, as I admit my smugness to you, my eyes tear up and my heart clenches.

God has never revealed sin to me in quite that way before or since. I was completely clueless, with not even an inkling of conviction ever before in this area. In fact, others had often mentioned my humility. I had owned up to many shortcomings, but pride didn't seem to be one of them. Talk about blind!

I remember having my quiet time on my bed, and God gave me a full-color shot of a prideful, superior heart that looked down on my husband, and all I could do was weep. Broken before God, I knelt and poured out my shame to Him. How had I missed this huge log in my eye? How had I spent years nurturing this attitude of condescension and never recognized it?

I have never felt so ashamed and so disappointed in myself. This wasn't as simple as confessing that I goofed, letting God change me, and moving on. I went through several months of gut-wrenching grief and brokenhearted mourning. I wept for days.

To this moment, I'm not sure why this sin above all others is so profoundly different, but I sensed God's displeasure deep in my spirit like never before. I know He hates pride. "There are six things the LORD hates, seven that are detestable to him: haughty eyes, a lying tongue, hands that shed innocent blood, a heart that devises wicked schemes, feet that are quick to rush into evil, a false witness who pours out lies and a man who stirs up dissension among brothers" (Prov. 6:16-19).

I wondered if my sinful attitude caused him to stumble and kept him away from Christ's outstretched arms.

Another reason is Dean. I wondered if my sinful attitude caused him to stumble and kept him away from Christ's outstretched arms. I can't bear to think of the damage my egotism may have caused.

I wrote in my journal, "True humility comes in my daily treatment of others, preferring them to myself and counting them better than me." Isn't that what Paul speaks of? "Your attitude should be the same as that of Christ Jesus: Who, being in very nature God, did not consider equality with God something to be grasped, but made himself nothing, taking the very nature of a servant, being made in human likeness. And being found in appearance as a man, he humbled himself and became obedient to death—even death on a cross!" (Phil. 2:5-8).

I thought humility was reflected in how highly I thought of myself. In a sense it is, because if I think better of myself than I think of someone else, I'm proud—not humble. True humility is revealed in our treatment of others and our attitudes toward them. This has been an awe-inspiring lesson for me. Self-righteousness sneaks in and grabs a foothold in our lives, often without our realizing that it's occurring.

WORDS, ACTIONS, AND BODY LANGUAGE

"I don't like my husband, but he doesn't have a clue," Gracie bragged to her girlfriend sitting next to her at a church luncheon.

Several of us around the table overheard, but since we weren't part of the conversation, we kept our opinions stifled. The truth was, however, that the only person Gracie was fooling was herself. Body language often speaks louder than words, and only a blind person would have failed to see how she felt about Mark.

When they sat together in church, she always angled away from him as she faced the pulpit. When Mark spoke, Gracie often interrupted or ignored him completely. If they ever accidentally made contact, she cringed. The looks she shot him were frosty, and her tone dripped with annoyance that he even shared the same planet.

I learned a valuable lesson from Gracie. Honoring my husband entailed much more than just saying the words. Respect is shown not only in the words I use but also in the tone I use and the expression with which they're said. For instance, if I say, "Yes, Dear," in a sweet tone with a smile on my face but roll my eyes, the observer perceives an entirely different message than when the same scenario takes place minus the roll of the eyes.

So honoring my husband entails all of me: my attitude, my words, my tone of voice, and my body language. Basically, it's difficult to pretend or to fool anyone when all those aspects play into venerating someone. I love the *Amplified Bible* version of Eph. 5:33—"Let the wife see that she respects and reverences her husband [that she notices him, regards him, honors him, prefers him, venerates, and esteems him; and that she defers to him, praises him, and loves and admires him exceedingly]." I'm fairly certain that if I'm following up on all that, there will be no room for pride in my heart.

Here's something else God brought to my attention, and it helped me to reframe my thoughts: God adores this man I'm married to, and He expects me to do the same. My goal is to become an A+ wife. This requires **a**ffirming, **a**ccepting, and **a**pproving of my husband. My words, actions, and attitudes should affirm that he's fearfully and wonderfully made—an incredible and individual work of God the Father. I need to accept him just who he is and just where he is. After all, isn't that what God does with me? I should express approval of him and love him as God loves me—unconditionally. Enormous freedom follows on the tailwind of adopting this Christlike attitude.

One way I can communicate these A+ ideals is by investing in my marriage. I must work at it every day and make it my highest calling and number one priority after God and above my children.

I love the following story I once heard my pastor tell. One of his neighbors had a beautiful, thick, green lawn—no small feat when you live in Arizona. Once when he commented to the man about his grass, the guy informed my pastor that his lawn could look exactly the same if he invested the same number of hours in watering, fertilizing, and weeding. Most of us want the thick turf without the work. A fabulous marriage is just like that lawn—it requires an investment of time and energy. It requires nurturing.

The second way I can communicate these A+ ideals is

by affection. We all need and want love, and touch is a powerful demonstration of love, even something as small as a pat on the hand. Numerous studies indicate that without touch humans as well as animals slowly die. Love is something we need to feel, see, and hear, so don't just tell him—show him. Affection affirms and shows approval.

For people like Gracie who don't even like the man they're married to, God can restore the old feelings if you'll let Him. When Dean and I went through the especially hard times in our marriage, I didn't like him much, and I'm sure the feeling was mutual. Through prayer and studying the Word, I decided to strive for a new friendship with my husband. It didn't happen overnight, because camaraderie requires time, planning, and even courage. At best, rebuilding was a risk. I struggled not to take him for granted anymore. Following Christ's example, I often died to myself and my wants, putting Dean's desires first. J. Allan Petersen, author of *The Myth of the Greener Grass,* instructs, "Positive action can have a positive effect on your feelings."[1] I discovered that the reaping made the sowing worthwhile.

My pastor tells another story about a disillusioned woman who just wanted out of her marriage. Deeply hurt by her husband's emotional neglect, she also wanted to have vengeance and to leave him with as much pain as he had caused her. A wise marriage counselor instructed her to spend the next six months serving her husband in every way possible. "Forget yourself completely, and do everything in your power to pamper and spoil this man. At the end of six months, when his love for you has been re-

---

1. J. Allan Peterson, *The Myth of the Greener Grass* (Wheaton, Ill.: Tyndale House, 1983), 199.

stored, leave him. You'll devastate him and cause tremendous pain."

When I focused on the plan of rebuilding, what I wanted took a backseat to the goal of restoration.

The woman followed her counselor's advice, but at the end of six months, as her counselor secretly knew would happen, she had fallen back in love with her husband, proving Petersen's words, "Positive action can change emotion." I, too, discovered that when I focused on the plan of rebuilding, what I wanted took a backseat to the goal of restoration. In Isaiah there's a promise that God can take the wasteland of our lives and make a beautiful Eden. I promise it's true. He did it for me. He'll do it for you too.

In summary, I must continually ask God to reveal pride and self-righteous attitudes in me. I also request that He make me aware of my presentation—not just what I say, but how I say it, my underlying heart attitude, and my body language. Pride destroys if we let the monster have free rein.

SCRIPTURAL EXAMPLES OF PRIDE

Isaiah—the son of Amoz and one of the greatest prophets—walked humbly with God. He had a tough job, speaking prophetic messages, woes, and judgments to sinful nations, and he even volunteered for the position. "Then [Isaiah] heard the voice of the LORD saying, 'Whom shall I send? And who will go for us?' And [Isaiah] said, 'Here am I. Send me!'" (Isa. 6:8).

I respect Isaiah. My response is usually, *Not me, Lord. Please, not me!* So in a sense Isaiah turned out to be the spreader of doom and gloom. People probably cringed when they saw this bearer of bad news headed in their direction. It was definitely a tough job, but God required somebody to speak His truth to those sinful nations.

As if the task weren't tough enough, God requested more of Isaiah. "At that time the LORD spoke through Isaiah son of Amoz. He said to him, 'Take off the sackcloth from your body and the sandals from your feet.' And he did so, going around stripped and barefoot" (Isa. 20:2). For three years Isaiah was naked and barefoot; the man laid aside his pride to honor what the Lord expected of him. How can I do less?

Jesus left us with two commands: Love God with everything in us, and love our neighbors. I must also lay aside any vestige of pride and love my husband as God intended. Isaiah's obedience afforded him the privilege of looking across the centuries to see the coming Messiah. Of all the great Hebrew prophets, Isaiah received the most complete picture of Jesus. He knew firsthand—years before the events took place—the story of Christ's birth, His mission, the titles He would carry, and the characteristic of who He was. Blessing always follows on the heels of obedience.

On the other hand, because of Saul's pride, the Lord rejected him as king. Let's check out 1 Sam. 15. God planned to punish the Amalekites for their past treatment of His chosen people. He sent Saul to destroy them and all their belongings, but Saul decided he had a better plan. He spared their king, Agag, and the best of the sheep and cattle.

His choice grieved the Lord, so God dispatched Samuel to speak to Saul, but Saul had traveled to Carmel to erect a monument in his own honor. (This man was once small in his own eyes but now considered himself worthy of a shrine.) When Samuel finally reached him, Saul greeted Samuel, boasting that he had carried out

God's instructions. Upon further scrutiny from Samuel, Saul admitted that his soldiers had spared the best, but only to sacrifice to God. Notice that he justified his disobedience, and his excuse bore a spiritual connotation.

When I fail to behave the way God tells me to, pride is at the core.

"But Samuel replied: 'Does the LORD delight in burnt offerings and sacrifices as much as in obeying the voice of the LORD? To obey is better than sacrifice, and to heed is better than the fat of rams. For rebellion is like the sin of divination, and arrogance like the evil of idolatry. Because you have rejected the word of the LORD, he has rejected you as king'" (1 Sam. 15:22-23). Partial obedience is still disobedience, and at the root of King Saul's decision lurked a heart filled with pride.

When I fail to behave the way God tells me to, pride is at the core. Anytime I choose my way over His, I'm ultimately saying I know better than God. When I treat my husband with anything but the utmost respect, pride has reared its ugly head again. I don't want to end up like Saul, rejected by God because I continuously insist on living life my way.

PONDERING GOD'S WORD

- "Pride goes before destruction, a haughty spirit before a fall" (Prov. 16:18).
- "When pride comes, then comes disgrace, but with humility comes wisdom" (Prov. 11:2).
- "By the grace given me I say to every one of you: Do not think of yourself more highly than you ought, but rather think of yourself with sober judgment, in accordance with the measure of faith God has given you" (Rom. 12:3).

- "If you think you are standing firm, be careful that you don't fall!" (1 Cor. 10:12).
- "Everyone who exalts himself will be humbled, and he who humbles himself will be exalted" (Luke 14:11).

Blessed Father,

Pride is so insidious. Please guard my heart. Make me aware of even the tiniest attitude of self-importance or self-righteousness. I never want to think more highly of myself than I do of Dean. I pray that the very thought of pride would continue to break my heart.

Remind me every day to affirm and accept my husband. Teach me to show approval and affection regularly. I desire to honor him in every way. Help me to hear how I sound to him and others. Make me aware of my nonverbal messages. I pray that my communication would clearly convey how dear Dean is to me and to You.

I yearn to be a humble servant like Isaiah and not prideful like Saul. In all honesty, though, I have a great propensity toward pride. Humility isn't natural and doesn't come easily. Change me, Lord, until my heart is like Yours, for there was no greater servant or portrait of humility than Christ Jesus, my Lord. May I be like Him. It's in His name I ask. Amen.

Listening to God's Voice

Ask God to show you new ways to serve your husband.
List them below.

_____

_____

_____

_____

_____

_____

_____

_____

_____

_____

_____

_____

_____

_____

_____

11
Thrilled Green
When a Friend's Husband Comes to Christ

"Hi," Hannah said. "It's good to see you. How's the family?" We hadn't seen each other for a couple of years, so meeting by chance at the mall seemed like a great opportunity to catch up. I filled her in on my family, and she caught me up on hers.

"Do you remember that Nikki married an unbeliever a couple of years ago?"

I nodded. How well I remembered! Her decision shocked and grieved our entire congregation. After all, Nikki grew up in a solid Christian home. Her dad was a deacon, and her mom was a Sunday School teacher. She had heard the truth her entire life, yet she chose to disobey God, her parents, and our pastor's advice. I braced myself for the news I was certain her mom was about to share—Nikki's choice had led to heartbreak and divorce.

"Chad accepted Christ a few weeks ago!" Hannah's face glowed with her happiness and relief over the news.

"What?" I nearly choked in disbelief. "You can't be serious!" Now embarrassed by my response, I have to admit I felt not joy but rather anger.

"Oh, but I am! He's going to church, planning to get baptized soon, and joined the new members' class."

"Wow." I know my one-word response held no enthusiasm, but honestly, I had an overwhelming urge to cry. A forced smile was all I could manage.

Hannah glanced at her watch, not appearing to notice all the negative emotions swarming through me at her *good* news. "Hey, I've got to run," she said in her upbeat tone. "Great seeing you. I knew you'd be thrilled about Chad since you nearly begged Nikki not to marry him. It all worked out fine." She gave me a quick hug and disappeared into the throng of shoppers.

I wasn't thrilled about Chad; I was angry. I race-walked toward my car, blinking furiously to keep my tears at bay. Once safely inside, I laid my head on the steering wheel and wept. *God, this isn't fair! I've faithfully walked with You for nearly two decades. How long, God? How long will I have to wait?*

For months I struggled to make logical sense of the justice system of God, and I have no answers for you.

I felt as if I had been punched in the stomach. *Nikki deliberately disobeyed, yet You blessed her. I don't understand! What happened to the principle of blessing following obedience—not disobedience?*

Nikki's news sent me in a downward spiral. I was furious with God. I didn't understand. Frankly, I still don't. So many women are in unequally yoked relationships not of their choosing. Nikki willfully married an unbeliever, and her story had a fairy-tale ending. For months I struggled to make logical sense of the justice system of God, and I have no answers for you. All I can tell you is what He revealed to me.

He is the Potter. I am the clay. He has every right to do as He pleases in my life, Nikki's life, and your life. His ways are not my ways. His thoughts are higher than my thoughts. He is the God of the universe—sovereign, just, and holy. He is Lord of Lords and King of Kings. I may not know the hows and whys, but I can rest assured that the plans He has for me are good because He tells me so in His Word. I came to the point at which I had to accept all of the above by faith. I might not agree with the "fairness" of God's decision, but I must accept His *authority* to make it.

Have you read Job 38 lately? Almighty God spoke to Job, and His words speak to me as well. He actually used them to break my heart and knock me off my prideful, self-made pedestal, where I demanded fairness. Let's look together at verses 1-13:

> Then the LORD answered Job out of the storm. He said: "Who is this that darkens my counsel with words without knowledge? Brace yourself like a man; I will question you, and you shall answer me. Where were you when I laid the earth's foundation? Tell me, if you understand. Who marked off its dimensions? Surely you know! Who stretched a measuring line across it? On what were its footings set, or who laid its corner-stone—while the morning stars sang together and all the angels shouted for joy? Who shut up the sea behind doors when it burst forth from the womb, when I made the clouds its garment and wrapped it in thick darkness, when I fixed limits for it and set its doors and bars in place, when I said, 'This far you may come and no farther; here is where your proud waves halt'? Have you ever given orders to the morning, or shown the dawn its place, that it might take the earth by the edges and shake the wicked out of it?"

God continues for three more chapters, and afterward Job admitted, "Surely I spoke of things I did not understand, things too wonderful for me to know" (42:3). And my response is the same—who am I to question God about things I don't understand, things too wonderful for me to know?

WHEN HER HUSBAND COMES TO CHRIST FIRST

Joy and I enjoyed each other's company and became close friends when I switched churches. We hung around together, sharing our Sunday pew, joining the same Bible study groups, and riding together to various women's functions. Church wasn't quite so lonely, knowing I had somebody there who cared about me. Then it happened—the phone call.

"Jim accepted Christ." I could barely understand her because she was crying so hard.

They'd been through a difficult time, and I was glad God brought fruit from their desert season. I truly felt happy, but a small part of my heart also struggled with envy, so instead of being tickled pink, I was thrilled green. A selfish little voice asked, "So now who will you sit with?"

If you have a friend whose husband comes to Christ, don't be surprised if you have a jumbled mess when it comes to your reaction.

My pastor's wife, Darleen, said, "I know just how you feel. When we were trying to have a baby and all our friends were successfully conceiving and we weren't, I was happy for them but a little sadder each time for me. Every round, protruding belly reminded me of something I might never have the pleasure of knowing. Feeling both happy and sad about Jim is normal. It's a bittersweet experience for you."

She was right, and her explanation helped me feel a little less guilty for my mixed emotions. She helped put everything in perspective, and even though Joy had been walking alone with the Lord only seven years, I didn't be-grudge her a Christian husband—it's just that I wanted one too. So if you have a friend whose husband comes to Christ, don't be surprised if you have a jumbled mess when it comes to your reaction. The bottom line, howev-er, is to work through your response and graciously ac-cept God's plan for your life and the lives of others. Sometimes that's the tough part.

SCRIPTURAL EXAMPLES

The disciple Peter struggled with the same issues. He wanted everything to be fair and square, and he wanted to make certain none of the other disciples got a better deal than he did. Picture Jesus and the disciples sharing breakfast at the edge of the Sea of Tiberias. This was the third time Christ appeared to them after His resurrection and before his ascension to heaven.

Once they had finished eating, Jesus asked Peter three times if he loved Him. By the third time, Peter was hurt. He said, "Lord, you know all things; you know that I love you."

Jesus responded, "Feed my sheep. I tell you the truth, when you were younger you dressed yourself and went where you wanted; but when you are old you will stretch out your hands, and someone else will dress you and lead you where you do not want to go" (John 21:17-18). Jesus was indicating the type of death Peter would experience in glorifying God.

Peter looked around and spotted John following them and asked, "Lord, what about him?" Jesus said, "If I want him to remain alive until I return, what is that to you? You must follow me" (vv. 21-22).

Jesus says the same thing to me. Regardless of what He does, what is it to me? I must follow Him. I can't wor-

ry about other people and how their lives work out—
that's between them and God.

But somewhere along the way, Peter quit worrying
about fairness and became courageous and immovable.
He became the rock that Christ prophesied He would
build His Church upon. Peter grew into a man who accepted God's plan for his life, even enduring his death, also upon a cross. Only, according to legend, he insisted on
being hung upside down, saying he wasn't worthy of the
same death Jesus died.

Jesus shared a parable in Matt. 20 about workers in a
vineyard. A landowner hired men early in the day to work
in his vineyard for a denarius. Three hours later, he hired
more men to do the same job for the same pay. Another
3 hours passed, and he hired more men to work for the
same pay. He repeated his action again in another 3
hours. Last, he hired men after the first group had already
worked 11 hours, but he paid them all the same—even
though some worked for only 1 hour and others for 12.

The men who worked the longest grumbled and com-
plained because they didn't think it was fair for laborers
who worked 1, 3, 6, 9, or 12 hours to all be paid the
same daily wage. No matter how long or short their work-
day was, each man pocketed one denarius. The landowner responded to their complaints by saying, "Don't I have
the right to do what I want with my own money? Or are
you envious because I am generous?" (v. 15).

He had every right to do what he did, but I'm certain
that if I had been one of the first hired, I would have been
unhappy too. God has the right to bless who He blesses
and curse who He curses, and frankly, it's none of my
business. I pray I'll also grow into a Peter, accepting not
only God's plan for me but also His plan for others without jealousy, envy, or question.

Pondering God's Word

- "Let us behave decently, as in the daytime, not in orgies and drunkenness, not in sexual immorality and debauchery, not in dissension and jealousy" (Rom. 13:13).
- "You are still worldly. For since there is jealousy and quarreling among you, are you not worldly? Are you not acting like mere men?" (1 Cor. 3:3).
- "A heart at peace gives life to the body, but envy rots the bones" (Prov. 14:30).
- "Where you have envy and selfish ambition, there you find disorder and every evil practice" (James 3:16).
- "Love is patient, love is kind. It does not envy, it does not boast, it is not proud" (1 Cor. 13:4).

Sovereign Lord,

Forgive me for questioning You, for throwing little fits when I don't get my way, and most of all forgive me for thinking I know best. You are the Potter. Mold me and make me just the way You want. Take my life, Lord, and do with it as You will. I trust You to work out Your very best plan for me.

Help me to be a true friend and rejoice when my friends have reason to rejoice and mourn with them when they have reason to mourn. Thank You for friends who understand my struggles and love me anyway.

Please change me the way You changed Peter to the point that other people's races don't tempt me to get off track. May I live the life You've chosen for me in such a way that You receive glory. In Christ's holy name I ask. Amen.

Listening to God's Voice

What is God saying to you during this time of waiting for
your husband to know Christ?

_____

_____

_____

_____

_____

_____

_____

_____

_____

_____

_____

_____

_____

_____

12

Great Expectations
When He Finally
Comes to Christ

And, God, please help my daddy to know You. Amen.

Six-year-old Holly's plea never failed to bring an ache to Jorie's heart. As they rose from their knees and she tucked Holly into her daybed under a frilly eyelet comforter, her silent petition echoed her daughter's: *Yes, may it be so, Lord Jesus.*

"Daddy will be home tonight," Jorie promised as she turned off the bedside lamp. "When you have breakfast tomorrow, he'll be there."

"I'm glad." Holly's voice resounded with pleasure. "He's been gone a long, long time. I missed him."

"Me, too, Baby. Me, too." Jorie pulled Holly's door partially shut and headed down the hall to her comfy chair in the family room. She would spend a few minutes with God until Dan arrived.

This had been Dan's longest business trip to date, and soon Jorie would feel his arms around her. He was a good man and a good provider. Their biggest problem was her newfound belief in Christ and his lack thereof. The past couple of years had strained their marriage as she settled into her faith walk. She knew that when he finally committed himself to Christ, everything would be perfect.

An hour later she heard the garage door open, laid her Bible aside, and ran for her husband's loving hug. He barely got out of the car before she plowed into him, wrapping lonesome arms around his waist. He returned the hug, almost squeezing the very breath from her body.

"Honey, it's so good to be home." His voice was tender, quiet, reverent. "I've got so much to tell you."

Jorie pulled back and studied him. "Dan, what's wrong?"

I asked Jesus to come into my heart, forgive my sins, and be my Lord. Isn't that what you wanted?

His eyes glistened with moisture, and his voice cracked with deep emotion. "Nothing's wrong, and everything's right. I accepted Christ a couple of days ago."

Tears of joy rolled down her cheeks amid her astonishment. Had she misunderstood? "You what?"

"You know—I asked Jesus to come into my heart, forgive my sins, and be my Lord. Isn't that what you wanted, what you've been praying for?" He appeared perplexed by her tears.

"Yes! Of course it is! I'm just—overwhelmed." She had prayed the prayer every day for two years, but somewhere deep inside she must have doubted Dan's conversion would ever happen. *Thank You, Jesus,* she whispered.

Dan wowed her with his charming smile, the one she had fallen in love with. Then he wiped the tears from her face with his thumbs and led her into the house. He pulled her down on the sofa next to him and wrapped his arm around her, pulling her close.

"Tell me what happened. Tell me everything!" Jorie couldn't wait to hear each detail of her answered prayer.

"At the last minute, Joe had to cancel going on the trip because of some family emergency, so Tristen stepped in to fill his shoes."

"Tristen? The head of operations? The guy who not only claims to be Christian but actually lives it?" Dan nodded. "Wow—talk about God's intervention! So he shared Christ and prayed with you?"

"Yes. I realized this whole religion thing had gotten between us, and when I contemplated how to fix our marriage, He used Tristen to help me see I was the one in need of fixing. So, Marjorie Elizabeth, will you take the new-and-improved Daniel Christopher to be your Christian husband?"

"I do," she promised.

I would like to tell you that Dan and Jorie lived up to her great expectations of the perfect Christian marriage, but unfortunately Jorie, in her cheerleader exuberance, pushed Dan too hard. She admits to having a different personality than he does, and when she became a Christian, she dove in, throwing caution to the wind. Jorie takes life by storm, while Dan wades in an inch at a time.

"When I became a Christian, I started having regular quiet times immediately, using a study book my church had given me. I attended church Sunday mornings, Sunday evenings, and Wednesday evenings for good measure. I loved to pray and took long prayer walks each day, often spending an hour or more conversing with God. I naturally assumed Dan's journey with the Lord would resemble mine. When it didn't, I pushed, prodded, and made strong suggestions."

Jorie's voice clouded over with sorrow as she continued. "If there were one thing I could redo in my life, it would be the six months following Dan's conversion. They were hell on earth and my biggest regret so far." She swallowed hard, a gulp reverberating over the phone line, and even though 1,500 miles separated us, I instinctively knew she was battling remorse and tears. I waited until she was ready to continue.

"If Dan was working on his computer, I would make a snide remark about not having time for God but always having time for work. If he decided to skip church for a football game, I would be furious and not speak to him for days. I made so many demands, he finally told me he was giving up on the Christian thing. There was no way he could live up to all my expectations.

"I was heartbroken, disillusioned, angry. I turned into a bitter woman. How had all my hopes and dreams dissolved into a puddle of misery and unhappiness? Dan started working late to avoid the ice queen he faced at home. The chasm between us grew until all we had was miles of stone-cold silence parked between us. The problems we faced before his conversion were small in comparison. Then came the day my life changed forever."

One afternoon Jorie's friend Katie dropped by. Katie's husband, Robert, worked in the same department as Dan, and Jorie and Katie had become good friends as well. Katie, always blunt and to the point, jumped right in. "I'm not sure how to tell you, but I think you need to know—Dan's having an affair." Her words pierced Jorie's heart, and Jorie felt as if she had been stabbed with a knife.

"What?" Jorie stumbled into a nearby chair. Feeling as if a huge weight rested on her chest, she struggled to breathe. She examined Katie's expression, hoping this was some cruel joke, but the sorrow on her best friend's face killed that wish. "You're sure?"

Katie nodded, tears welling in her eyes. "If it were Robert, I'd want to know."

"Part of me didn't want to know," Jorie confessed. Now she had to face facts, make decisions. Feeling numb, she couldn't think. She ached to be alone and cry. Nausea assaulted her stomach. *Help me, God. Please, help me,* she cried out silently. "With who?" she whispered, feeling her world spinning out of control.

"Lauren." Lauren—the name all the office wives dreaded. Her reputation as a single woman who preyed on married men haunted each of them.

"He told Robert that while you constantly beat him down, Lauren offered him a safe haven from your criticism. She admires him. He said you never say a kind word anymore and that you shrink away from his touch." Katie paused, knowing her words were devastating Jorie.

"Robert thinks that as Dan's vulnerability increased, Lauren moved in for the kill. He resisted at first, but when your relationship got worse and worse, he gave in to adultery."

Adultery—what an ugly word! Katie hugged Jorie, and they cried together. "I'll never forget her next words," Jorie said.

"Remember—temptation is out there, looking exactly like what we think we need and want. At a time when Dan needed acceptance, encouragement, and appreciation, Lauren offered all that plus more." Jorie could only nod, devastated by the news.

"I'm taking Holly home with me tonight so you'll have time to think. Dan won't be home from his business trip until tomorrow afternoon. You need to figure things out. You need to pray." Katie took charge, and Jorie went into the bathroom to pull herself together before hugging Holly good-bye.

Alone in the house, Jorie grabbed her Bible and fell on her face before God. *How could this have happened?* she wondered. Mulling over the past few months, all the signs were there with glaring reality. How had she missed them? No wonder Dan forgot their 10th anniversary; his mind and heart were elsewhere.

"I wanted to condemn Dan, but as I spent the night broken before God, He convicted me instead. At home Dan had faced nagging, criticism, and complaints, not always as direct hits but often disguised in sarcasm and humor. I cringed when he touched me, and his advances came less often, ending altogether several months before his affair became known. For me, his disinterest was a huge relief since I felt so angry with him—that is, until I realized Lauren satisfied his needs.

"Divorce lurked on my horizon like a bad dream. I never imagined myself single again. I don't know where I thought we were headed, but certainly not the end of our life together. I opened my Bible, reading through all the passages on divorce, marriage, and adultery. I cried out to God in confusion, *Help me to know the right thing to do!*

"Sleep refused to free me from the horror, so I spent the night alternating between crying, praying, and reading the Word. I kept going back to Mark 10:5—'It was because your hearts were hard that Moses wrote you this law.' The passage referred to divorce, and I had to ask myself, *Is my heart so hard that that's the only answer?* Yes, my heart had been hard, uncaring, and self-centered, but on the brink of losing Dan, my heart broke before God. He showed me I had much responsibility for the mess our lives were in. I was broken by my own sin; I could do nothing but forgive Dan for his affair.

When one of our spouses comes to Christ, it's up to Him to grow him.

"A few days later after a weeping apology from my husband, I looked him in the eye and said, 'I can forgive you because God has forgiven me.' At that moment I realized it was the most Christlike act I had ever committed, and I could feel God's pleasure."

Happily, I can report that through much prayer and hard work, God restored Jorie and Dan's marriage. Sadly, Dan still desires nothing to do with church, his Bible, or God. Jorie largely blames herself for that and desires to caution other women to pray, not push. When one of our spouses comes to Christ, it's up to Him to grow him. We're not His mouthpiece, so we must avoid any sort of nagging, preaching, or subtle hints.

I know in my own daydreams I've often imagined the white-picket-fence life we'll live after Dean decides to follow Christ. I've thought of how wonderful it will be to have a man to pray with me and for me. I've written a storybook ideal in my head that could be quite far from what might actually transpire. The truth is, none of our husbands will turn into super-Christians overnight, and many of them never will. I have to remember how long it's taken me to reach this point and how very, very far I still have to go on the journey toward Christlikeness.

I can't possibly know what will transpire after the big decision is made, but it will behoove me to keep my feet firmly planted in reality. Expectations have a way of disappointing, and disappointment breeds discontentment. But acceptance equals peace.

For several years I tried to press Dean into the Christian mold. I was miserable, he was miserable, and frustration plagued us both. My great expectations almost destroyed our marriage. Through that era, I learned that a picture is still worth chapters of words, so I pray to be a portrait of Christ for my husband to see—not a sermon for him to hear. *Live it! Don't say it!* I've also discovered that God is more willing to change me than my circumstances.

I do yearn for the day Dean and I will walk this path of faith together, but I acknowledge that change can come only from God. I strive to enjoy who he is now—today. But I pray for the man he'll someday be.

SCRIPTURAL EXAMPLES

Let's look at two examples from Scripture: Queen Esther and Sarah. Queen Esther received word from her cousin Mordecai that Haman, a nobleman given a seat of honor by the king, was plotting to have all the Jews killed. He had promised to pay the royal treasury for their destruction. Mordecai begged Esther to intervene for the sake of her people.

Instead of rushing headlong into the situation, Queen Esther asked the Jewish people to fast for three days and three nights. She and her maids fasted as well. Only after they all sought the Lord would she consider going to the king. When she did go before the king, the request she made was that he and Haman come to a feast.

Notice that she was in no hurry. Her second request was for the king and Haman to attend a banquet on the following day. There she exposed Haman's evil plan to annihilate the Jews, starting with Mordecai. Haman's life ended on the very gallows he had prepared for Mordecai.

Sarah, on the other hand, did not attempt to seek the Lord. She decided her husband, Abraham, should sleep with her maidservant. Since the Lord hadn't given Sarah children, she would build a family another way. Abraham did sleep with Hagar, his wife's maid, and she conceived a son. Sadly, the two women ended up hating each other, and Sarah's plan went from a bad idea to disaster.

Sadder still, Ishmael, the child born to Hagar, was the father of the Arab people—the same people who have warred against Israel, God's chosen nation, for several millennia. Sarah's choice to take things into her own hands has had far-reaching effects.

I want to be an Esther, not a Sarah. I hope to seek the Lord and let Him direct me rather than plowing ahead with my own expectations, because it's obvious that human answers don't work. They only make a bigger mess.

Pondering God's Word

- "The LORD longs to be gracious to you; he rises to show you compassion. For the LORD is a God of justice. Blessed are all who wait for him!" (Isa. 30:18).
- "You expected much, but see, it turned out to be little" (Hag. 1:9).
- "I waited patiently for the LORD; he turned to me and heard my cry" (Ps. 40:1).
- "Those who hope in the LORD will renew their strength. They will soar on wings like eagles" (Isa. 40:31).
- "Maintain love and justice, and wait for your God always" (Hos. 12:6).

Father,

I've so often put my expectations on my husband and then faced disappointment. Teach me instead to place my expectations in You alone. Teach me to wait for You to work. I confess, I frequently plan and run ahead of You. I also confess the times I tried to fix Dean and mold him into my ideal of who he should be. Forgive me, Father.

I do look for and long for the day my husband commits his heart and life to You, but I need to guard my mind from plotting and dreaming about the way things might be. Teach me to live today and hope for tomorrow without writing the script.

It is with anticipation and a grateful heart that I look forward to the future. You are so good, so kind, so loving. I trust You with whatever lies ahead. May my days as a spiritually single woman bring You glory. In Christ's name I pray. Amen.

Listening to God's Voice

What attitudes are you harboring toward your husband that might be hindering his becoming a believer?

_____

_____

_____

_____

_____

_____

_____

_____

_____

_____

_____

_____

_____

_____

_____

_____

13

Road to Contentment
Accepting Where God Has Us

The new year lurked just around the corner. Ready for something new in my life and feeling weary, I decided this would be the year. I would pray with more boldness, more faith, and more belief. *Look out, God, because I plan to be one pesky prayer warrior this year!*

In truth, I was still doing everything the same except that I had this new unwavering determination that this would be the year. (I was fooling myself because my determination wasn't going to equal my husband's salvation.) I cruised through the first couple of months boldly claiming Dean's salvation.

The first week of March, I went to a ladies' retreat in Prescott, Arizona. On the last day, the speaker talked about Paul's being content in chains. "Are you content with whatever you're chained to in this life?" she asked, pausing for effect.

In His still, small voice, God whispered in my heart, *Jeri, will you be content if Dean never walks with Me?*

I'm not saying that God told me my husband won't ever surrender to Christ. What I *am* saying is that God asked if I would be content if he never does.

The question broke my heart. I sat in that A-framed chapel and cried. I couldn't even sing the closing song. For 20 years I had prayed, knowing that someday, somehow Dean would come wholeheartedly to Christ. The past two months I had pumped up that hope, confidently declaring this would be the year.

With one softly whispered challenge from God, all hope diminished. I grieved the rest of the day and many days that followed. Could I do it? Could I walk this spiritually single trek another 20 or 30 years? My heart ached at the prospect.

The reason I started praying boldly in the first place was because weariness had crept in. Twenty-one years was a long season. I wrote in my journal a couple of months before, "I've spent my whole marriage unequally yoked. Please let me spend the rest with a committed Christian husband." I longed for that, ached for it, but maybe it would never be.

My future looked bleaker than it had in ages. Every time I considered the possibility of doing this another two decades, I wept.

The grief over the following weeks weighed heavily upon me as I buried my hopes for any time soon. My future looked bleaker than it had in ages. Every time I considered the possibility of doing this another two decades, I wept. I honestly didn't know if I could.

About six weeks later, while at a writers' conference in California, the Lord gave me the opportunity to write this book. I write fiction and wasn't even considering nonfiction, but when the editor spoke to me about the project, I knew God wanted me to write this book. The Holy Spirit washed over me in confirmation.

At the very lowest point in my journey as a spiritually single married woman, God asked me to share my voyage with you. Never in all my years did I feel so inept to encourage other women in my shoes. How could I bring hope when I had none?

I wrestled with God over the next couple of months, often wondering if I would have the strength to write this book or to keep on going alone. I continued to mourn the loss of my dream and count the cost of the road before me.

While I worked through a Bible study on patience, God began to bring me through the valley and help me understand what transpired in my life the last few months.

The Greek word *hypomonē* is the most common definition of patience. It means to persevere, remain under, bear up under, showing the quality of character that does not allow one to surrender to circumstances or succumb under trial. The word speaks of endurance in relationship to things or circumstances.

Hope has a very strong and crucial tie to this sort of patience. Hope is the desire of some good with the expectation of obtaining it. It's what inspires us to endure the things or circumstances in our lives. When God asked me if I would be content if I spent the rest of my life united to an unbeliever, I lost my hope. Suddenly I had no expectation of obtaining my deepest longing. The world became bleak indeed, but God taught me several valuable lessons through this experience.

Lesson One: I can't just decide I've had enough of the way things are and pray harder, bolder, and longer to achieve my way in my time. I must accept God's timing, His sovereignty, and the fact that Dean has a free will.

Lesson Two: I must live my life one day at a time. I was worrying about 20 years from now. God wisely offers only enough strength and provision for today. "Do not worry about tomorrow, for tomorrow will worry about itself. Each day has enough trouble of its own" (Matt. 6:34).

Lesson Three: God has faithfully been with me every step of the way these past 22 years, and He'll continue to faithfully lead me forward. I can count on Him no matter what the future does or doesn't hold. "Trust in the LORD with all your heart and lean not on your own understanding" (Prov. 3:5).

Bonus Points: A few weeks later, God led me to this passage:

> Praise be to the God and Father of our Lord Jesus Christ, the Father of compassion and the God of all comfort, who comforts us in all our troubles, so that we can comfort those in any trouble with the comfort we ourselves have received from God. For just as the sufferings of Christ flow over into our lives, so also through Christ our comfort overflows. If we are distressed, it is for your comfort and salvation; if we are comforted, it is for your comfort, which produces in you patient endurance of the same sufferings we suffer. And our hope for you is firm, because we know that just as you share in our sufferings, so also you share in our comfort *(2 Cor. 1:3-7)*.

Our hard times are for each other! My trials are to bring you hope, comfort, and encouragement. My prayer is that you've found those on the pages of this book. May God bless you as you live for Him.

Listening to God's Voice

Write a prayer of surrender, giving your husband's future to God.

_____

_____

_____

_____

_____

_____

_____

_____

_____

_____

_____

_____

_____

_____